Anonymous

Personnel of the Senate and House of Commons

Eighth Parliament of Canada

Anonymous

Personnel of the Senate and House of Commons
Eighth Parliament of Canada

ISBN/EAN: 9783337150549

Printed in Europe, USA, Canada, Australia, Japan

Cover: Foto ©Suzi / pixelio.de

More available books at **www.hansebooks.com**

PERSONNEL

OF THE

SENATE

AND

HOUSE OF COMMONS

EIGHTH PARLIAMENT OF CANADA

ELECTED JUNE 23, 1896.

PORTRAITS AND BIOGRAPHIES OF THE MEMBERS

Montreal:
JOHN LOVELL & SON
1898

INTRODUCTION.

The object of the following pages is to afford in the most condensed and convenient form a biographical and pictorial sketch of the Personnel of the Senate and House of Commons of the Eighth Parliament of Canada.

In the series of biographies here presented will be found the most important facts and dates in the history of every member of the two Houses of Parliament.

The information given has been collected from the most reliable sources, and carefully verified and edited.

The accompanying portraits are photo-gravure reproductions of the best and most recent photographs procurable.

MAIN PARLIAMENT BUILDING.

EASTERN DEPARTMENTAL BUILDING.

WESTERN DEPARTMENTAL BUILDING.

LANGEVIN DEPARTMENTAL BUILDING.

Ishbel Aberdeen

RT. HON. SIR WILFRID LAURIER, P.C., K.C.M.G.
(Prime Minister and President of the Council.)

Sir Wilfrid Laurier, Prime Minister of Canada, was born in the village of St. Lin, County of L'Assomption, Province of Quebec, on the 20th of November, 1841, his father being the late Carolus Laurier, Provincial Land Surveyor, a descendant of an old French family. He was educated at L'Assomption College and at the University of McGill, where, in 1864, he took the degree of B.C.L. He was called to the Bar the same year, and on October 11, 1880, was appointed a Q.C. His first parliamentary experience was as a member of the Quebec Assembly, to which he was elected in 1871 for the Counties of Drummond and Arthabaska. He represented that constituency in the local House until 1874, when he resigned to contest the same seat for the House of Commons, in which he was successful. In 1877 he entered Hon. Mr. Mackenzie's Administration as Minister of Inland Revenue. At the by-election held through his acceptance of office he was defeated, but found a seat in Quebec East, through the resignation of the Hon. I. Thibaudeau, and retained his portfolio until the resignation of the Mackenzie Administration in 1878. He was re-elected for Quebec East at the general elections of 1878, 1882, 1887, 1891 and 1896, in which year he was also elected for Saskatchewan, but chose to stand by his old constituency. On the retirement of the Hon. Edward Blake, in 1888, from the leadership of the Liberal Party, Mr. Laurier was unanimously chosen for the position, which by his winning personality and commanding eloquence he has vitalized from a dormant faction into a living force. On the resignation of Sir Charles Tupper's Administration in 1896, Sir Wilfrid was sent for by Lord Aberdeen to form a Government, himself as Prime Minister and President of the Council. Sir Wilfrid, like a great many of Canada's public men, has had some journalistic experience, having been at one time editor of a paper called *Le Défricheur*. At the celebration of Queen Victoria's Jubilee in 1897, Sir Wilfrid represented Canada with such dignity and grace as to command the admiration of all classes in the two countries. On that occasion Her Majesty bestowed on him the rank of K.C.M.G., and he was also the recipient of many other tokens of appreciation from different cities in England and Scotland. He also visited Paris, and was specially honored by the President of the French Republic and by several public bodies. During his tour, which was in the nature of a triumphal procession, he delivered several notable addresses, and, for a time at least, attracted universal attention to Canada, which there is good reason to believe will benefit greatly in the future from the masterly way in which he set forth her claims as a field for the capitalist and emigrant. Sir Wilfrid was married on May 13, 1868, to Miss Lafontaine, who shares with him the esteem of the whole Canadian people.

HON. SIR R. J. CARTWRIGHT, K.C.M.G.
(Minister of Trade and Commerce.)

The Hon. Sir Richard John Cartwright, K.C.M.G., was born at Kingston, December 4. 1835, being the son of the late Rev. R. D. Cartwright, chaplain to the Forces of Kingston, and is a grandson of Hon. Richard Cartwright, a U. E. loyalist, and who was a member of the first Parliament of Upper Canada, which met in 1792, and continued to hold a seat in that body to the time of his death in 1815. He was educated at Trinity College, Dublin. He married in August, 1859, Frances, eldest daughter of the late Col. Alex. Lawe, H. E. I. C. S. He was President of the late Commercial Bank of Canada. He is the author of a pamphlet on the Militia question (1864). November 7, 1873, he was sworn of Privy Council, and appointed Minister of Finance, which office he held until the resignation of the Mackenzie Administration in October, 1878. He went to England in 1874 on public business, and again in 1875 and 1876. He sat in the Canadian Assembly for Lennox and Addington from 1863 until the time of the Union. He was elected to the Commons for Lennox at the general election of 1867, also at general election of 1872, also upon his appointment to office and by acclamation at general election of 1874. He was defeated at the general election of 1878, and was elected for Huron on the resignation of the sitting member November 2, 1878. He was an unsuccessful candidate for the County of Wellington at the general election of 1882. In December, 1883, he was elected by acclamation for South Huron on the resignation of the sitting member. He was re-elected for his present seat at the general elections of 1887, 1891 and 1896. He was created a K.C.M.G. in 1879. Upon the formation of the Laurier Government he was again sworn of the Privy Council, and was appointed Minister of Trade and Commerce, July 13, 1896. A Liberal.— *Kingston, O.*

HON. R. W. SCOTT, Q.C., LL.D.
(Secretary of State.)

The Hon. Richard William Scott was born at Prescott, February 24, 1825. He is the son of the late W. J. Scott, Esq., M.D., who served on the medical staff of the army in the Peninsular war, and who subsequently came to Canada and became Registrar of the County of Grenville. Ont., and Sarah Ann, daughter of the late Capt. A. McDonnell, of Matilda, Dundas, Ont. He was educated at Prescott. He married Mary Ann, daughter of the late Mr. J. Heron, of Ottawa. At the Easter Term, 1848, he was called to the Bar of Upper Canada, and was appointed Q.C. in 1867. In 1852 he was elected Mayor of Ottawa. In December, 1871, he was elected Speaker of the Ontario Assembly, but resigned on his appointment to the Executive Council as Commissioner of Crown Lands for that Province, which position he held until November, 1873, when he was sworn of the Queen's Privy Council. He was Secretary of State from January, 1874, until October, 1878, when he resigned with the Mackenzie Administration, of which he was a member. He was called to the Senate in March, 1874. He represented Ottawa in the Canada Assembly from 1857 until 1863, when he was defeated, and held the same seat in the Ontario Assembly from the general election of 1867 to November, 1873, when he resigned. In 1863 he prepared and carried the Separate School Law of Ontario. He was appointed LL.D. University of Ottawa in 1889. He was Leader of the Opposition in the Senate until July, 1896, when he became Secretary of State in the Laurier Administration. A Liberal.—*Ottawa*.

HON. DAVID MILLS, LL.B.
(Minister of Justice.)

The Hon. David Mills was born in the Township of Oxford, County of Kent, Ont., March 18, 1831. He is the son of Nathaniel Mills, formerly of New York State, who emigrated to Nova Scotia, and again removed to Upper Canada. He was educated at the Public Schools and at Michigan University, where he received the degree of LL.B. In December, 1860, he married Miss M. J. Brown. In 1883 he was called to the Bar, and was appointed Q.C. in 1896. He was elected to the Commons for Bothwell in 1867, and has held that seat ever since. He was sworn of the Privy Council, and appointed Minister of the Interior in the Mackenzie Government from 1876 until the resignation of the Government in 1878. He was first returned to Parliament in 1867, and was re-elected in 1872, 1874 and 1878. In 1882 he was again a candidate, but was unable to take his seat until declared by the judgment of the Supreme Court to have been improperly deprived of the seat. He was re-elected in 1887 and 1891, but defeated in 1896. He was appointed to the Senate in November, 1896. Appointed Minister of Justice November 18, 1897. A Liberal—*London, O.*

HON. SIR L. H. DAVIES, Q.C., K.C.M.G.
(Minister of Marine and Fisheries.)

The Hon. Sir Louis Henry Davies, Q.C., was born in Charlottetown, P.E.I., on May 4, 1845. He is the son of the Hon. Benjamin Davies, and is a grandson of Nathan Davies, Esq., who in 1809 came to Prince Edward Island. He was educated at the Prince of Wales College and at the Central Academy. He married at St. Eleanors, P.E I., in July, 1872, Susan, fourth daughter of the late Rev. Dr. A. V. G. Wiggins. He was called to the Bar of Prince Edward Island in 1866, and was appointed a Q.C., November 26, 1880. For many years he held the office of President of the Merchants' Bank of Prince Edward Island. He was Counsel for the Tenantry before the Land Commission of Prince Edward Island, presided over by the Right Hon. H. C. Childers, and he was also one of the Canadian Counsel before the International Fishery Commission at Halifax in 1877. He was Solicitor-General of Prince Edward Island in 1869, and also in 1872 and 1873, and was Leader of the Opposition in the Legislative Assembly until September, 1876, when he became Premier and Attorney-General. In March, 1879, his Administration resigned. He sat in the Legislative Assembly of Prince Edward Island from November, 1872, until the general elections held in 1879, in which year he was defeated. At the general elections held in 1882 he was first elected to the House of Commons, and was re-elected at the general elections held in 1887, 1891, and 1896. He was sworn of the Privy Council, and was appointed Minister of Marine and Fisheries on July 13, 1896. On his acceptance of office he was re-elected by acclamation. On the occasion of Her Majesty's Diamond Jubilee he was created Knight Commander of the Order of St. Michael and St. George. A Liberal.—*Charlottetown, P.E.I.*

HON. F. W. BORDEN, M.D.
(Minister of Militia and Defence.)

The Hon. Frederick William Borden, M.D., was born in Cornwallis, King's County, N.S., May 14, 1847. He is the son of the late Dr. Jonathan Borden, who for thirty years followed his profession in his native County, King's. He was educated at King's College, Windsor, in Arts, where he took his degree of A.B. in 1866, and at Harvard Medical School, Boston, in Medicine, where he graduated an M.D. in 1868. He has been married twice: first, on October 1, 1873, to Julia M., daughter of J. H. Clark, Esq., of Canning ; and, second, on June 13, 1884, to Bessie B. Clark, of Canning. He was agent of the Bank of Nova Scotia at Canning from September, 1882, until May, 1891, in which year the Agency was closed. Since then he has been agent at Canning of the Halifax Banking Co. He was first elected to Parliament at the general elections held in 1874, and was re-elected at the general elections held in 1878. He was an unsuccessful candidate at the general elections held in 1882, and was re-elected at the general elections of 1887 and in 1891. He was unseated in November, 1891, and was re-elected February 13, 1892, and again at the general elections held in 1896. In July, 1896, he was sworn of the Privy Council and was appointed Minister of Militia and Defence. He was re-elected by acclamation on his appointment to office. A Liberal.—*Canning, N.S.*

HON. WM. MULOCK, Q.C., LL.D.
(Postmaster-General.)

HON. S. A. FISHER, B.A.
(Minister of Agriculture.)

The Hon. William Mulock was born in the Village of Bond Head, Township of West Gwillimbury, County of Simcoe, January 19, 1843. He is the second son of the late Thomas Homan Mulock, M.D., of King's County, Ireland, and Mary, daughter of the late John Cawthra, formerly of Yorkshire, England, who settled in Newmarket, County of York, and was Reform Member in the Legislative Assembly of Upper Canada for Simcoe in 1829. He was educated at the Newmarket Grammar School and at the University of Toronto, where he graduated in Arts in 1863. He was called to the Bar of Ontario in 1868. He married, May 25, 1870, Sarah Ellen Cawthra, daughter of James Crowther, of Toronto. In 1890 he was appointed a Q.C. by the Ontario Government. He was elected a member of the Senate of the University of Toronto in 1873 and 1878, and Vice-Chancellor, University of Toronto, in 1881, and has held that position ever since. For several years he was one of the Examiners in and Lecturer on Equity for the Law Society of Upper Canada. He was first elected to Parliament at the general elections of 1882, and was re-elected in 1887, 1891 and 1896. He was sworn of the Privy Council and appointed Postmaster-General July 13, 1896, and was re-elected by acclamation on his acceptance of office. A Liberal.—*Yorkville, O.*

The Hon. Sydney Arthur Fisher, B.A., was born in Montreal on June 12, 1850. He is the son of Dr. Arthur Fisher, of Montreal, whose grandfather came from Dunkeld, Scotland, to Canada. He was educated at the High School of Montreal and at McGill College of the same place, and subsequently at Trinity College, Cambridge, England, from which place he graduated a B.A. He is unmarried. He is by occupation a farmer, and is a J.P. for the District of Bedford. For the last five years he has been Vice-President of the Province of Quebec Dairy Association. He is one of the founders and has been Vice-President for two years of the Provincial Fruit Growers Association, and is President of the Ensilage and Stock Feeding Association of Montreal, and is a director of the Brome County Agricultural Society. For a period of fifteen years he has been a member of the Council, and is also one of the Vice-Presidents for Quebec of the Dominion Alliance for the Prohibition of the Liquor Traffic. At an election held in October, 1880, he was an unsuccessful candidate for his present seat, following the death of the sitting Member. He was first elected to Parliament at the general elections held in 1882; he was re-elected at the general elections held in 1887, and was defeated at the general elections held in 1891. He was re-elected at the general elections held in 1896. On July 13, 1896, he was sworn of the Privy Council and was appointed Minister of Agriculture. A Liberal.—*Knowlton, Q.*

HON. J. I. TARTE.
(Minister of Public Works.)

Hon. Joseph Israel Tarte was born at Lanoraie, County of Berthier, P. Q., in 1849, and was educated at the College of L'Assomption. He first commenced business as a notary, but followed that profession for two years only, when he merged into journalism, which field he found more congenial to his taste. Mr. Tarte soon came to be recognized as a trenchant and virile, yet withal graceful writer, and in his position as editor of *Le Canadien* established a reputation as a progressive journalist. Entering politics, he was elected to the Legislative Assembly of Quebec for Bonaventure from February 23, 1877, until the general elections of 1881, when he retired. Mr. Tarte was elected to Parliament for Montmorency, but in 1891 the election was declared void, and he subsequently stood for the constituency of l'Islet at a by-election, when he was successful. At the general elections of 1896 he unsuccessfully contested the County of Beauharnois Having been sworn of the Privy Council and appointed Minister of Public Works on July 13, 1896, he sought the suffrages of his present constituents at a by-election, the vacancy being caused by the appointment of the member-elect to the Senate. A Liberal.—*Ottawa*.

HON. R. R. DOBELL.
(Minister without Portfolio.)

The Hon. Richard Reid Dobell was born in Liverpool, England January 27, 1836; his father, Mr. George Dobell, being a gentleman of independent means. He received his education at Liverpool College, and early in life showed a great adaptability for business. Coming to Canada in 1857, he engaged in business as a timber merchant at Quebec, which port then enjoyed a comparative monopoly in the exportation of lumber. Mr. Dobell grew to be one of the most extensive exporters in the trade, and his firm has all along maintained an enviable reputation on both sides of the Atlantic. Outside of his immediate business, Mr. Dobell is largely interested in several important public companies, attention to which leaves him with little leisure time on his hands ; still social duties are not neglected, and personally he is very popular among all classes of society in Quebec, where he is best known and appreciated for his business integrity and generous disposition. Mr. Dobell was married to a daughter of the late Sir David Q. Macpherson, K.C.M.G., of Toronto. At the by-election of 1895, Mr. Dobell contested his present seat, but was unsuccessful. At the general elections of the following year (1896) he was returned by a handsome majority, and on the formation of Sir Wilfrid Laurier's Administration was, on July 13 of the same year, appointed a Cabinet Minister without portfolio. A Liberal.—*Quebec*.

HON. W. S. FIELDING, P.C.
(Minister of Finance.)

The Hon. Wm. Stevens Fielding, P.C., was born at Halifax, N.S., November 24, 1848, and is of English descent. He was educated at Halifax. He married on September 7, 1876, Hester, daughter of Thomas A. Rankine, Esq., of St. John, N.B. He is by occupation a journalist, and was for many years connected with the *Halifax Morning Chronicle*. He is a governor of Dalhousie University, and is president of the St. George's Society of Halifax. At the convention of the Liberal Party, which was held at Halifax, in 1882, for the formation of a new Administration after the resignation of the Thompson Government, the offices of Premier and Provincial Secretary were offered to him, but were declined. December 22, 1882, he entered the Administration of the Hon. W. T. Pipes. He resigned in May, 1884. On July 15, 1884, on the retirement of the Hon. Mr. Pipes, he was called upon to reorganize the Administration, and he held the offices of Premier and Provincial Secretary from July 28, 1884, to July 18, 1896, on which date he resigned, and on July 20, 1896, was sworn of the Privy Council and appointed Minister of Finance in the Laurier Administration. He sat in the House of Assembly of Nova Scotia for Halifax from the general elections held in 1882 until July 18, 1896. He was first elected to the House of Commons in July, 1896, on the appointment of Mr. F. G. Forbes, the member-elect, to an office under the Crown. A Liberal.—*Halifax, N.S.*

HON. A. G. BLAIR, Q.C., LL.D.
(Minister of Railways and Canals.)

The Hon. Andrew George Blair, Q.C., LL.D., was born in Fredericton, New Brunswick, March 7, 1844. He married, October 31, 1866, Annie E., eldest daughter of George Thompson, Esq., of the Educational Department, Fredericton. He was educated at the Collegiate School, Fredericton. In April, 1866, he was called to the Bar. He was first elected to the House of Assembly at the general elections held in 1878. On a petition being filed against his return he resigned his seat, and on the issue of a new writ was re-elected November 14. 1878. He was Leader of the Opposition until the close of the term. He was re-elected at the general elections held in 1882. On March 3, 1883, he formed an Administration, and was re-elected on his acceptance of office as Attorney-General, March 24, 1883. He was re-elected at the general elections of 1886 and also at the general elections of 1890, and again at the by-election held October 23, 1890. At the general elections of 1892 he was defeated for York, but was re-elected for Queen's, November, 1892, upon the resignation of the member elect, Mr. Hetherington. He was re-elected at the general elections held in 1895. In 1896 he resigned the Premiership and his seat in the House of Assembly. He was sworn of the Privy Council and was appointed Minister of Railways and Canals in the Liberal Administration of Sir Wilfrid Laurier, July, 1896. He was elected to his present seat in the Commons, August 25, 1896, on the appointment of Mr. G. G. King, the member elect, to an office of emolument under the Crown, A Liberal.—*St. John, N.B.*

HON. C. SIFTON, Q.C.
(Minister of the Interior.)

The Hon. Clifford Sifton was born in the Township of London, Middlesex County, Ont., March 10, 1861. He is the son of the Hon. J. W. Sifton, at one time Speaker of the Legislative Assembly of Manitoba, and Kate Watkins, both of whom came from Ireland and settled in Middlesex County. He was educated at the London High School and Victoria University, from which Institution he received the gold medal. He married August 14, 1884, Elizabeth Arma, daughter of Mr. H. T. Burrows, formerly of Ottawa. He studied law in the office of the Hon. S. C. Biggs, Q.C, in Winnipeg, and began the practice of his profession in Brandon, where he became senior partner in the firm of Sifton, Philip & Cameron. He was elected a member of the Board of School Trustees, and in 1886 was appointed solicitor for the Western Judicial Board. He held a seat in the Manitoba Legislative Assembly for North Brandon, and in 1891 he was appointed a member of the Executive Council as Attorney-General, and was also in charge of the Departments of Education and Crown Lands, which positions he held until 1896, when he resigned. November 17, 1896, he was sworn of the Privy Council and became Minister of the Interior. On November 27 he was elected by acclamation to the House of Commons for Brandon. A Liberal.— *Brandon, Man.*

HON. C. A. GEOFFRION, Q.C., D.C.L.
(Minister without Portfolio.)

The Hon. Christophe Alphonse Geoffrion was born at Varennes. County of Verchères, 23rd of November, 1843, his father being Felix Geoffrion, and his mother Catherine Brodeur. He is a younger brother of the late Hon.F. Geoffrion, who was a member of the Mackenzie Administration. He was educated at the College of St. Hyacinthe and at McGill University. He graduated a B.C.L. in 1866, and was admitted to the Bar in June of same year. He was *Batonnier* of the Bar, Section of Montreal, in 1884-1885. He was appointed a Q.C. on February 18, 1887. The degree of Doctor of Civil Law was conferred upon him at McGill University in 1893. He married, in 1870, Eulalie, eldest daughter of the late Chief Justice Sir A. A. Dorion. He was first elected to the Dominion Parliament for Verchères at a by-election necessitated through the death of his brother, the Hon. Felix Geoffrion, in April, 1895, and was re-elected at the last general elections for Chambly and Verchères in 1896. Sworn of the Privy Council and became a member of the Laurier Administration without portfolio, August, 1896. A Liberal.—*Montreal*.

HON. WM. PATERSON.
(Minister of Customs.)

The Hon. William Paterson was born in Hamilton, Ont., September 19, 1839, being the son of James Paterson, Esq., formerly of Aberdeen, Scotland, who arrived in Canada some years previously. He was educated partly in Hamilton, finishing in Caledonia under Dr. Ferrier. Mr. Paterson was married in September, 1863, to a daughter of T. C. Davies, Esq., of Brantford. He is an indefatigable worker with great business capacity, by the exercise of which he built up the extensive concern known as the Brantford Steam Confectionery and Biscuit Works, of which he was proprietor. Mr. Paterson has devoted much of his time to the public service, and among the minor offices held by him was that of Town Councillor, 1868, Deputy-Reeve, 1869, 1870 and 1871, and Mayor 1872. He was first elected to Parliament for South Brant, at the general elections of 1872, and was again re-elected five consecutive terms for the same constituency, namely, at the general elections of 1874, 1878, 1882, 1887 and 1891. At the general elections of 1896 he again offered himself for re-election, and was unsuccessful; but, having been appointed Controller of Customs in the Laurier Administration, he contested the County of North Grey at a by-election held in August of the same year, the vacancy being caused by the death of the member elect, Mr. Clark, and was successful. By an Act of Parliament passed at the Session of 1897 he became Minister of Customs instead of Controller. A Liberal,—*Brantford, O.*

HON. SIR H. G. de LOTBINIERE.
(Minister of Inland Revenue.)

The Hon. Sir Henry Gustave Joly de Lotbinière was born in France, December 5, 1829, being the son of the late Gaspard Pierre Gustave Joly, Esq., Seigneur de Lotbinière and of Julia Christin, daughter of the late Hon. M. E. G. A. Chartiere de Lotbinière, who, from 1794 to May, 1797, was Speaker of the Quebec Assembly, and was afterwards a member of the Legislative Council of Quebec. He was educated in Paris. He married the daughter of Hammond Gowan, Esq., of Quebec. In March, 1855, he was called to the Bar of Lower Canada. He was appointed a Q.C. March 9, 1878. In January, 1877, he was offered a seat in the Dominion Cabinet as Minister of Agriculture, but declined it. Upon the dismissal of the De Boucherville Government in March, 1878, by Lieut.-Governor Letellier de St. Just, he became Premier and Commissioner of Public Works. His Ministry resigned on October 30, 1879. From 1879 until 1883 he was Leader of the Opposition. He sat for Lotbinière in the Canadian Assembly from the General Elections of 1861 until the time of the Union, when he was elected by acclamation to the House of Commons and the Legislative Assembly. He continued to sit in both Houses until the General Elections of 1874, in which year he retired from the Commons and continued to sit in the Legislative Assembly till he resigned in 1885. He was elected to his present seat at the General Elections of 1896. Upon the formation of the Liberal Government by Sir Wilfrid Laurier, he was appointed Controller of Inland Revenue, July 9, 1896. By an Act of Parliament passed at the Session of 1897 he became Minister of Inland Revenue instead of Controller. In May, 1895, he was created a K.C.M.G. A Liberal.—*Quebec.*

HON. C. FITZPATRICK, Q.C.
(Solicitor General.)

The Hon. Charles Fitzpatrick was born in the City of Quebec, December 19, 1853. He is the third son of Mr. John Fitzpatrick, who was an extensive lumber merchant of Quebec. He was educated at the Quebec Seminary, Ste. Ann's College, and afterwards at Laval University in the Law Faculty, where he won the Dufferin Medal in 1876. He was called to the Bar in the same year, and became a member of the firm of Andrews, Caron & Fitzpatrick. He married, May 20, 1879, Corinne, daughter of the late Hon. R. E. Caron, who was Lieut.-Governor of the Province of Quebec at the time of his death, and sister of Sir Adolph P. Caron, K.C.M.G. In 1878 he was appointed Crown Prosecutor for the District of Quebec during the Administration of the Hon. Mr. Joly, and again in 1886. He was engaged as Counsel for the defence of Louis Riel, who in 1885 was tried and condemned to death. In 1891 he was offered the Attorney-Generalship in the DeBoucherville Ministry, but declined. He was appointed Q. C. in 1893. He held a seat in the Legislative Assembly of Quebec from 1890 until June, 1896, when he resigned his seat to run for the Commons, and was elected for Quebec County. He was appointed Solicitor-General of Canada in the present Administration on July 13, 1896. A Liberal.—*Quebec.*

LORD STRATHCONA AND MOUNT ROYAL.
(High Commissioner for Canada in the United Kingdom.)

Lord Strathcona, better known as Sir Donald A. Smith, was born in Morayshire, Scotland, in 1820, and educated there. He came to Canada when quite a youth, and entered the service of the Hudson's Bay Company rising gradually step by step until he attained the position of Director and afterwards President, Resident Governor and Chief Commissioner in Canada, and was elected in 1888 to the position of Governor of that Corporation. It is safe to affirm that no man living knows more of that extensive tract of country known as the North-West Territories than Lord Strathcona. He has led a busy and active life, and during his long career has been closely identified with most of the great commercial enterprises which have done so much to build up Canada, and at the present time is President of the Bank of Montreal. He represented Winnipeg and St. John in the Manitoba Assembly from the first meeting of that body in 1871, until January, 1874, when he resigned. Sat in the Commons for Selkirk on the admission of Manitoba into Confederation in 1871, and was re-elected at the general elections of 1872, 1874 and 1878, which latter, upon petition, was voided. He was returned for Montreal West in 1887, and sat continuously for that constituency until Parliament was dissolved in April, 1896. Sworn of the Privy Council and appointed High Commissioner April 24, 1896. Lord Strathcona's many acts of benevolence are well known. In conjunction with Lord Mount-Stephen he built and endowed the Royal Victoria Hospital in the Queen's Jubilee year, 1887, and his munificent gifts to McGill College (of which he is Chancellor) has been the means of raising that institution to a foremost position among the seats of learning of this Continent. His latest gift in this connection is the building of the new "Donalda College" for the higher education of women. On the celebration of her "Diamond Jubilee," Her Majesty the Queen was graciously pleased to bestow a peerage upon Sir Donald under the title of Lord Strathcona and Mount Royal. A Liberal-Conservative.—*Montreal.*

THE SENATE.

HON. C. A. P. PELLETIER, C.M.G., B.C.L., Q.C.
(Speaker of the Senate.)

The Hon. Charles Alphonse Pantaleon Pelletier was born at River Ouelle, Kamouraska County, January 22, 1837. He is the son of J. M. Pelletier and Julia Painchaud. He was educated at Ste. Anne's College and Laval University, where he received the degree of B.C.L. in 1858. He was married twice: first, to Susanne, daughter of the late Hon. C. E. Casgrain, M.L.C., and, second, to Virginia A., daughter of the late Hon. M. P. DeSales La Terriere, M.D. He is by profession an advocate, and was appointed Q.C. in 1879. He has been Syndic and *Batonnier* of the Quebec Bar. He is a director of the Quebec Fire Assurance Company and retired Major of 9th Batt. of Voltigeurs de Quebec. He was elected for Kamouraska in 1869, and was re-elected at the general elections of 1872 and 1874. He, at the same time, was representing the Quebec-East Division in the Quebec Legislative Assembly until dual representation was abolished. He was sworn of the Privy Council in 1877 as Minister of Agriculture in the Mackenzie Administration, and held that office until 1878, when he resigned with his colleagues. Was President of the Canadian Commission for the Paris Universal Exhibition of 1878. He was created a C.M.G. in October, 1878. He was called to the Senate February 2, 1877, and was appointed Speaker of the Senate, July, 1896. A Liberal.—*Quebec*.

E. J. LANGEVIN, N P.
(Clerk of the Senate.)

Edouard Joseph Langevin was born at Quebec, October 1, 1833, and educated at the Seminary there, and St. Mary's College, Montreal. He is the fourth son of the late Jean Langevin, Esq., of Quebec, and a brother of His Lordship the late Bishop of Rimouski and of the Hon. Sir Hector L. Langevin, K.C.M.G. He has been twice married; first to a daughter of the late Hon. James Armstrong, C.M.G., Chief Justice of St. Lucia and Tobago, West Indies; second, to Marie Albina Giroux, of Montreal. Mr. Langevin was admitted as a Notary, L.C., 3rd December, 1858; practised for some years as a notary, and was a member of the Chamber of Notaries for the District of Quebec. He served as a volunteer officer during the "Trent" affair, and became Major of the 9th Batt. "Voltigeurs de Quebec," retiring in 1865, retaining rank. On January 4, 1865, he was appointed Clerk of the Crown in Chancery, Can., and to the same office for the Dominion July 5, 1867; Deputy Registrar-General, July 1, 1868; Under-Secretary of State, July 9, 1873; Secretary of the Civil Service Board, 1876; Clerk of the Senate, January 25, 1883; a Commissioner to administer the oath of allegiance to Members of the Senate, January 31, and Master in Chancery, February 7, 1883.—*Ottawa*.

J. de ST. D. LeMOYNE.
(Sergeant-at-Arms.)

Juchereau de St. Denis LeMoyne was born July 13, 1850, and is the eldest son of the late Robert A. LeMoyne, Esq., Clerk of the Senate. He received his early education at the Seminary of Quebec, and subsequently went to St. Mary's College, Montreal, where he made rapid progress, distinguishing himself in various branches of study. He was married on April 29, 1875, to Margaret Louise, daughter of William Mackay, Esq., of Ottawa. Mr. LeMoyne was appointed Acting Sergeant-at-Arms in May, 1869, and was promoted in 1873 to his present position, and was further appointed Clerk of French journals.—*Ottawa*.

HON. M. ADAMS, Q.C.
(Northumberland, N. B.)

The Hon. Michael Adams was born in Douglastown, Parish of Newcastle, N.B., August 13, 1845, and is of Irish descent. He was educated in Douglastown. He has been married twice: first, in 1869, to Miss Catherine L. Patterson, and second, on November 29, 1882, to Miss Nealis. He was called to the Bar of New Brunswick on October 14, 1868, and was appointed a Q.C. in February, 1891. He was Surveyor-General of New Brunswick and also a member of the Executive Council from July, 1878, until February, 1882. He held a seat in the Legislative Assembly of N. B. from 1870 to 1874, and also from 1878 to 1887, when he resigned to run for the Commons, but was defeated. He was first elected to the House of Commons for Northumberland, N.B., at the general election held in 1891, and continued to sit until January, 1896, when he was called to the Senate. A Conservative.—*Newcastle, N.B.*

HON. J. C. AIKINS, P.C., LL.D.
(Home.)

The Hon. James Cox Aikins was born in the Township of Toronto, Peel, Ont., March 30, 1823, and is of Irish descent. He was educated at the University of Victoria College, Cobourg. He was married in 1845 to Miss M. E. J. Somerset. He represented Peel in the House of Assembly from 1854 until 1861. He was a member for the Home Division in the Legislative Council from 1862 until the Union. He was Secretary of State from December, 1869, until November, 1873, the date that the Macdonald Government resigned. He was reappointed Secretary of State in 1878, and Minister of Inland Revenue in 1882. He was called to the Senate in May, 1867, and sat until May, 1882. He was Lieut. Governor of Manitoba and Keewatin from 1882 to 1888. He was reappointed to the Senate in January, 1896. A Liberal Conservative.—*Toronto, Ont.*

HON. G. W. ALLAN, P.C., D.C.L., F.R.G.S., F.Z.S.
(York.)

Son of the late Hon. William Allan, of Moss Park, Toronto. Born in Toronto, January 9, 1822. Educated at U.C. College. Married, 1st, Louisa Maude, third daughter of the late Hon. Sir J. B. Robinson, Bart.; 2nd, Adelaide Harriet, third daughter of the late Rev. T. Schreiber, formerly of Bradwell Lodge, Essex, Eng. Called to the Bar U. C. Hilary Term, 1846. Is Chief Commissioner of the Canada Company, President of the Western Canada Loan Company and Vice-President of the North American Life Assurance Company. Is Lieut.-Colonel of the Regimental Division of East Toronto, Chancellor of the University of Trinity College and a D.C.L. of the same institution. Honorary President of the Ontario Society of Artists and President of the Council of the Ontario School of Art. Is a Fellow of the Royal Geographical Society and Member of the Zoological Society of England. Is President of the Upper Canada Bible Society. Was Mayor of Toronto in 1855. Sat for York Div. in the Legislative Council from 1858 until Confederation. Was speaker of the Senate March 17, 1888, until Feby., 1891. Appointed a member of the Privy Council for Canada May 30, 1891. A Conservative.—*Moss Park, Toronto.*

LIEUT. COL. HON. J. F. ARMAND
(Repentigny.)

The Hon. Joseph Francois Armand was born at Rivière des Prairies, P.Q., December 14, 1820. He is of French descent, his grandfather being a Royalist. He is a son of Lieut.-Col. Francois Armand and Marie Louise Vincent. He was educated at the St. Hyacinthe College. He was married in 1855 to Alphonsine, daughter of the late Amable Simard, Esq., M.D. He is Lieut.-Col. of the 16th Batt. Montreal Militia. He sat for Alma division in the Legislative Council of Canada from 1859 until the time of the Union. Called to the Senate by Royal Proclamation in May, 1867. A Conservative. — *Rivière des Prairies, Q.*

HON. W. J. ALMON, M.D.
(Halifax.)

The Hon. Wm. Johnson Almon was born in Halifax, January 27, 1816. He is the son of the late Hon. Wm. Almon, M.D., and is a grandson of Wm. James Almon, assistant surgeon of the Royal Artillery in New York in 1776. He was educated at King's College, Windsor, and received the degree of B.A. in 1834, also studied medicine in the Universities of Edinburgh and Glasgow, and graduated an M.D. at the latter University in 1838. Is a trustee of the N. S. Building Society, also a Governor of King's College, Windsor, and is Consulting Physician to the Halifax Hospital and Dispensary. Married in 1840 to Elizabeth Lichtenstein, daughter of late Judge Ritchie, of Annapolis, N.S. Has held the offices of President of Halifax Club and Surgeon of the Halifax Field Battery of Artillery. Was elected to the Commons for Halifax County in 1872. Appointed to the Senate April 15, 1879. A Conservative.—*Halifax, N.S.*

HON. G. T. BAIRD.
(Victoria.)

The Hon. George Thomas Baird was born at Andover, N.B., November 3, 1847. He is the eldest son of George Baird, and is of Scotch descent. He was educated at Carleton County Grammar School. He was married November 12, 1879, to Ida T., daughter of Captain D. W. Sadler, of St. John, N.B. He held a first class certificate from the Normal School of New Brunswick, and for six years he taught a Superior School and was also Postmaster from 1878 until 1882. He has been engaged in a successful business as a lumber merchant and general dealer at Perth Centre, N.B., since the year 1874. He was first elected to the New Brunswick Legislature in 1884. He was appointed to the Legislative Council of that Province on April 11, 1891, and continued to sit in the House until its abolition. At the general election held in 1892 he was again elected to the local House, where he sat until he was called to the Senate, June 19, 1895. A Conservative.—*Perth Centre, N.B.*

HON. G. B. BAKER, M.A., Q.C.

(Bedford)

The Hon. George Bernard Baker was born at Dunham, Q., January 26, 1834, and is the third son of the late William Baker, Esq., who sat for Missisquoi in the Lower Canada Assembly from 1834 until 1837. Was educated at the University of Bishop's College, Lennoxville, graduating in 1855. Is a trustee of the University of Bishop's College. He married in 1860 Jane Percival, eldest daughter of Peter Cowan, Esq., of Cowansville. Held a seat in the Executive Council, and was Solicitor-General of Quebec from January 27, 1876, until March 12, 1878. Held his seat in the Commons from July, 1870, until 1874, when he resigned. At the general elections of 1878 and 1882 he was re-elected to the Commons; defeated in 1887 and at by-election in 1888, and re-elected in 1891, sitting until January 7, 1896, when he was appointed to the Senate. A Conservative.—*Sweetsburg, Q.*

HON. JOSEPH BOLDUC.

(Lauzon.)

The Hon. Joseph Bolduc was born at St. Francois de la Beauce, June 22, 1847. He is the son of Captain A. Bolduc, a descendant of Louis Bolduc, who came to Canada in 1668 as the *Procureur du Roi*. He was educated at Ste. Marie College and at Laval University. Was married in October, 1873, to Miss M. G. A. Mathieu, at St. Francois. Is engaged in business as a lumber merchant, and a notary by profession. He has been Warden of the County of Beauce, and Mayor of the Parish in which he resides ; also President of the School Trustees, director of the county Agricultural Association, and also of the Levis and Kennebec Railway. Has been successful in the promoting of the Tring & Megantic Railway, which affords Quebec and Levis the shortest route to the Maritime Provinces and New England. He represented Beauce from October, 1876, to October, 1884, when he was called to the Senate. A Conservative.—*St. Victor de Tring, Q.*

HON. J. H. BELLEROSE.
(DeLanaudiere.)

Hon. Joseph Hyacinthe Bellerose was born at Three Rivers, P.Q., July 12, 1820, and educated at the Colleges of Nicolet and St. Hyacinthe. He was married in 1847 to a daughter of Lieut.-Col. Armand. Holds the rank of Lieut.-Col. commanding Laval Reserve Militia. In 1859 he was commander of the whole force in Military District No. 8. In 1858 Sir E. W. Head, then Governor-General, offered him, by desire of Her Majesty the Queen, a captaincy in the 100th, or "Prince of Wales Royal Canadian Regiment," which he accepted, but shortly afterwards, for private reasons, he resigned. After the death of Sir George E. Cartier he was offered a portfolio in the Cabinet but declined. He represented Laval in the Canadian Assembly from 1863 until the Union, and from that event in the Dominion Parliament until called to the Senate, October 16, 1873. He also represented Laval in the Quebec Assembly from the Union until the general elections of 1875, when he retired. During the whole of that period he was Chairman of the Contingent Committee, and is credited with having effected great reductions in the House expenditure. A Conservative.—*St. Vincent de Paul, Q.*

HON. JOHN DOBSON.
(Lindsay.)

The Hon. John Dobson was born in the County of Fermanagh, Ireland, September 8, 1824, and is the son of John Dobson and Mary Henry. He was educated at the Public Schools. After residing in Toronto for a few years he removed to Lindsay. He was elected Mayor of Lindsay by acclamation in 1873, and also to the office of President of the Board of Trade. He has been President of the South Victoria Agricultural Society and Chairman of the School Board for several years. He was also President of the South Victoria Conservative Association for over 25 years. He was called to the Senate, February 23, 1892.—A Conservative, pure and simple.—*Lindsay, O.*

HON. LIEUT.-COL. C. A. BOULTON.
(Marquette.)

The Hon. Lieut.-Col. Charles Arkel Boulton was born at Cobourg, Ont., April 17, 1841. He is the son of Col. D'Arcy Boulton, of the 4th Regiment Prince of Wales Canadian Dragoons, who married Emily Heath, daughter of Brigadier-General Heath, of the Hon. East India Company's service, in 1839. He was educated at the Upper Canada College, Toronto. He is by occupation a farmer. He was an officer of H. M. 100th Regiment from 1858 to 1868, and Major of the 46th Batt. East Durham from 1868 to 1881. He held the offices of Reeve of Lakefield, Ont., Warden of the County of Russell, Man., and Registrar of the United Counties of Shoal Lake and Russell. He was a candidate in Marquette, Manitoba, in the general elections of 1887, but was defeated by 58 in a poll of 4,500 votes. He accompanied the surveying party under Surveyor-General Dennis to the Northwest in 1869. He was present in the Selkirk settlement during the troubles of 1869-1870, and was imprisoned with the party in Fort Garry, February 19, 1870, as they were returning to their homes after effecting the release of the prisoners who were taken in Dr. Schultz's house on December 6. He was imprisoned and sentenced to be shot, but was reprieved at the solicitation of Sir Donald A. Smith and Archdeacon McLean, and was released March 20 with the rest of the prisoners after the arrival of Archbishop Taché. Commanded Boulton's Scouts during the Rebellion of 1885, in the North West Field Force, under General Sir Fred. Middleton. Lieut.-Col. Boulton was one of the Military Contingent which represented Canada at the Diamond Jubilee of Queen Victoria, and took part with the Canadian Contingent force in the notable procession that accompanied Her Majesty to St. Paul's Cathedral. He was appointed by Sir John Macdonald as a member of the Canadian Parliament in the Senate, December 10, 1889. A Liberal-Conservative and Free Trader.—*Shellmouth, Man.*

HON. LIEUT.-COL. SIR M. BOWELL, K.C.M.G.
(Hastings.)

Was born at Rickinghall, Suffolk, England, December 27, 1823. Came to Canada with his parents, 1833. Married, Dec., 1847, Harriet Louisa, eldest daughter of the late J. G. Moore, Esq., of Belleville. Was a Major 49th Batt. of Volunteer Rifles, and served upon the frontier during the American Rebellion in 1864, and in 1866, during the Fenian troubles; retired as Lieut.-Col. Has been Vice-President of the Dominion Editors' and Reporters' Association; Vice-President of the Agricultural and Arts Association of Ontario, and President of the Belleville & North Hastings Railway. Was Editor and Proprietor of the Belleville *Daily and Weekly Intelligencer* newspaper for a lengthened period; and has also been President of the Ontario Press Association. Held the Chairmanship of the Board of School Trustees, Belleville, for eleven years, and was for eight years Right Worshipful Grand Master of the Provincial Grand Orange Lodge of Ontario East. Elected Most Worshipful Grand Master and Sovereign of the Orange Association of B.A., 1870—an office he continued to hold until he resigned in 1878. Was President of the Tri-Annual Council of the Orange Association of the World. Moved the resolution for the expulsion of Louis Riel from the Commons, which was carried April 16, 1874. Was a special Commissioner to Australia, in 1893, for the promotion of closer trade relations between Canada and that country; a member of and Chairman of the Colonial Conference, held in Ottawa in 1894, and Commissioner for Canada in the Pacific Cable Conference held in London, 1896. Created K.C.M.G., Jan. 1, 1895. Sworn of the Privy Council and appointed Minister of Customs, Oct. 19, 1878, and held that office until the death of the Prime Minister, Sir John A. Macdonald, June 6, 1891. Was also Minister of Customs in the Administration of Sir John Abbott, from June 16, 1891, to Jan. 24. 1892, when he was transferred to the Dept. of Militia and Defence, where he continued until the resignation of Sir John Abbott, Nov. 24, 1892. On the creation of the new Department of Trade and Commerce, he was entrusted with the organization of that Department and accepted that portfolio in the Administration of Sir John Thompson, Dec. 5, 1892. Was Leader for the Government in the Senate until the death of Sir John Thompson, when he formed an Administration, and became Prime Minister, Dec. 13, 1894, and President of the Council, Dec. 21, 1894. Resigned, April 27, 1896. Is now Leader of the Opposition in the Senate. Sat in the House of Commons from 1867 to 1892. Resigned his seat in the Commons, and was called to the Senate, Dec. 5, 1892. A Conservative. —*Belleville, O.*

HON. C. E. BOUCHER de BOUCHERVILLE, M.D., C.M.G.
(Montarville.)

The Hon. Chas. Eugene Boucher de Boucherville was born at Boucherville, Que., May 4, 1822. He is the son of the late Hon. P. Boucher de Boucherville. He was educated at St. Sulpice College, Montreal, and afterwards at Paris. He married, first, Suzanne, daughter of R. L. Morrough, Esq., of Montreal, and, second, Miss C. Lussier, of Varennes. He sat for Chambly in the Assembly from 1861 until the time of the Union. Is a member of the Legislative Council, Quebec. He became Premier, Secretary, Registrar, and Minister of Public Instruction in September, 1874, and in January, 1876, he was removed to the Department of Agriculture and Public Works. In 1878 he was dismissed by Lieut.-Governor Letellier de St. Just. In December, 1891, he was again made Premier, and continued in that office until December, 1892, and then resigned. He was created a C.M.G. in May, 1894. He was appointed to the Senate in February, 1879. A Conservative.—*Boucherville, Q.*

HON. L. J. FORGET.
(Sorel.)

The Hon. Louis Joseph Forget was born at Terrebonne, March 11, 1853. His ancestors originally came to Canada from Normandy, in France, about 1600. He was educated at Masson College. He was married, May 2, 1870, to Marie Raymond, of Montreal. He is in business as a banker and stock broker. He is also President of the Street Railway Company, the Richelieu & Ontario Navigation Company, and the Montreal Stock Exchange, and he holds the office of Vice-President of the Board of Governors of Laval University. He was called to the Senate in June, 1896. A Conservative.—*Montreal.*

HON. G. A. DRUMMOND,
(Kennebec.)

Hon. George Alexander Drummond was born at Edinburgh, Scotland, in 1829, and was educated at the famous High School and equally famous University of that city. He came to Montreal in 1854, and was married three years later to a daughter of the late John Redpath, Esq., after whose death he again married, this time to Miss Grace Julia Hamilton, a daughter of the late A. Davidson Parker, Esq. Hon. Mr. Drummond is not at present in business, but is extensively interested in a large number of important financial and commercial institutions and manufacturing and mining companies. At present he is Vice-President of the Bank of Montreal, President of the Art Association of Montreal, in which he takes a warm interest, and is a liberal patron of the fine arts. Mr. Drummond is also an ex-President of the Board of Trade. He was called to the Senate, December 1, 1888. A Conservative.—*Montreal*.

HON. R. B. DICKEY, Q.C.
(Amherst.)

The Hon. Robert Barry Dickey was born at Amherst, Nova Scotia, November 10, 1811, and is the only son of the late R. M. Dickey, M.P. for Cumberland County for 16 years. He was educated at the Windsor Academy. He married in October, 1844, Mary Blair, third daughter of the late Hon. Alexander Stewart, C.B. He was called to the Bar of Nova Scotia in January, 1834, and to that of New Brunswick in 1835, and was appointed a Q.C. in 1863. He has since retired from active practice. In 1858 and 1865 he was one of the delegates from the Nova Scotia Government to England in the matter of the Intercolonial Railway and Federation, and in 1864 to the Charlottetown and Quebec Union Conference. He was Consular Agent for the United States at Amherst, and has also been a director of the Nova Scotia Electric Telegraph Co. He was a member of the Legislative Council of Nova Scotia from 1858 to the time of the Union. He was appointed to the Senate by Royal Proclamation in May, 1867. A Conservative.—*Amherst, N.S.*

HON. T. A. BERNIER.
(St. Boniface.)

The Hon. Thomas Alfred Bernier was born at St. George de Henryville, County of Iberville, P.Q., August 15, 1844 He is of French descent, and is the son of the late Thomas Bernier and Julia Letourneau. Was educated at the College of St. Hyacinthe, P.Q. He was married in August, 1871, to Julia Malvina, daughter of A. I. Demers, of Henryville. He was then engaged in journalism. Is by profession an advocate, and practised for some years in St. John d'Iberville, P.Q., and subsequently, in 1880, he removed to Manitoba. He was Superintendent of Education for the Catholic schools in Manitoba from 1881 to 1890, when the Catholic schools were abolished. Registrar of the University of Manitoba from 1881 to 1893. A member of the Executive Committee of the Provincial Agricultural Board, and Chairman of the Eastern Judicial District Board. Has been Mayor of St. Boniface ; Commissioner to revise the municipal law, also Commissioner to enquire into the working of the law in connection with the sale of half breed lands, and president of various societies. Appointed to the Senate in October, 1892, where he is championing the cause of the minority on the Manitoba school question. A Conservative.—*St. Boniface, Man.*

HON. G. G. KING.

The Hon. George Gerald King was born at Springfield, King's County, N. B., December 11, 1836, and is the son of Malcom King, of Fintry, Scotland, and of Elizabeth Hickson, of Miltown, Ireland. He was educated at Springfield. Was married on October 23, 1860, to Esther, daughter of Ebenezer Briggs. By occupation a lumber merchant. Was Warden of Queen's County in 1877. Sat in the House of Commons from 1878 until 1886. At the last election mentioned, he received a majority of the votes, but lost his seat through the action

of the Returning Officer. Re-elected at the general elections of 1891 and also of 1896. Called to the Senate in December, 1896. A Liberal.—*Chipman, N. B.*

HON. SIR JOHN CARLING, P.C., K.C.M.G.

The Hon. Sir John Carling was born in the Township of London, County of Middlesex, January 23, 1828. He is the youngest son of the late Thomas Carling, Esq., of London, Ont. He was educated at the common schools. He was married to a daughter of the late Henry Dalton, Esq., of London, September 4, 1849. He is a Director and President of the firm of Carling & Co., brewers. He was a member of the London City Council from 1854 to 1858. He represented London in the old Parliament of Upper and Lower Canada from 1857 to 1867. In 1862 was a member of the Government as Receiver-General. Was Commissioner of Agriculture and Public Works from 1867 to 1871, and held a seat as a member of the Legislature until 1872. He held a seat in the Commons to 1874, and was re-elected in 1878. He was sworn in Postmaster General and Member of the Privy Council in 1882, until 1885, when he became Minister of Agriculture, and continued so until 1892. He was appointed Senator in 1891, but resigned in 1892, and re-elected to the Commons, and sat there until 1896, when he was again called to the Senate. He was created a K.C.M.G. in 1893. A Liberal-Conservative.—*London, O.*

HON. M. H. COCHRANE.

(Wellington.)

The Hon. Matthew Henry Cochrane was born at Compton, Nov. 11, 1823. He is of Irish descent, the family having come from the North of Ireland, and is the son of Mr. James Cochrane, a Quebec merchant. He is extensively engaged as a cattle importer and breeder. He was formerly a member of the firm of Cochrane, Cassils & Co. of Montreal. He is a trustee of the Lennoxville University, and holds several other public offices, such as Director of the Eastern Townships Bank, and of the Waterloo and Magog Railway Co., President of the Cochrane Ranch Co., the British American Ranch Co., and the Bigelow Heel Co. He was appointed to the Senate in October, 1872. A Conservative.—*Hillhurst Station, Q.*

HON. DAVID WARK.
(Fredericton.)

The Hon. David Wark was born in the vicinity of Londonderry, Ireland, February 19, 1804. He is of Scotch descent, both of his parents having come from Scottish families that settled in Ulster about the 17th century. He came to New Brunswick in 1825. He married Annie Elizabeth, daughter of Isaac Burpee, Esq., of Sunbury, N.S. He is a retired merchant. He is a member of the Senate of the University of New Brunswick. From 1858 until 1862 he was a member of the Executive Council of New Brunswick, and was also Receiver-General, which office he resigned on taking his seat in the Senate in 1867. He sat in the New Brunswick Assembly, for the County of Kent, from 1843 until 1851, when he was appointed to the Legislative Council of that Province, in which body he remained until the time of the Union. In May, 1867, he was called to the Senate by Royal Proclamation. A Liberal.—*Fredericton, N.B.*

HON. P. A. DeBLOIS.
(LaSalle.)

The Hon. P. A. DeBlois was born in the city of Quebec, October 15, 1815. He is engaged in business as a farmer. He was married to Miss Geneviève Lefebvre. He formerly did business as a merchant in Quebec. He has held the office of Mayor of the Parish of Beauport. He is an uncle of Hon. Sir A. P. Caron, M.P. Was called to the Senate, February 13, 1883. A Conservative.—*Mastai, Q.*

HON. GEO. A. COX.

(Saugeen.)

The Hon. George Albertus Cox was born in Colborne, Northumberland County, Ont., May 7, 1840, and is of English parentage. He was educated at the public and grammar schools there. In 1856, he was appointed operator for the Montreal Telegraph Company at Colborne, and in 1858, he removed to Peterborough to take a similar position with that Company. He married in May, 1862, the second daughter of the late Daniel Hopkins, of Peterborough. From 1858 until 1871, he was actively engaged in the life and fire insurance and real estate business in Peterborough, and in the latter year he was appointed President and General Manager of the Midland Railway of Canada, which position he retained until the road became part of the G. T. R. in 1884. He is at the present time President of the following Institutions: Canadian Bank of Commerce, Central Canada Loan & Savings Company, Western Assurance Company, British America Assurance Company, and is also a Director of the Canada Life Assurance Company, Toronto General Trusts Company, Canadian General Electric Company, and various other financial and industrial institutions. He was Mayor of Peterborough for several years. In 1871, he was elected for West Peterborough in the Commons, but the election being declared void, a new one was held and he was defeated by a majority of one. He was appointed to the Senate in November, 1896. A Liberal.—*Toronto, O.*

HON. JAMES DEVER.

(St. John.)

The Hon. James Dever was born at Ballyshannon, Ireland, May 2, 1825. Came to New Brunswick, with his parents, and settled at St. John, and became possessed of property. Was appointed to the Senate, March 14, 1868. Married Margaret Morris, November 25, 1853. There are nine children by this marriage. A Liberal.—*St. John, N.B.*

HON. C. E. CASGRAIN, C.M., M.D.
(Windsor.)

Hon. Charles Eusèbe Casgrain, C.M., M.D., was born in the city of Quebec, August 5, 1825, and both on his father's and his mother's side is descended from old and distinguished French ancestry. His father was the late Hon. Chas. E. Casgrain, a lawyer in Quebec, who represented Cornwallis in the Lower Canada Assembly from 1830 to 1834, was a member of the Special Council of Lower Canada from 1838 to 1840. and at the time of his death held the office of Assistant Commissioner of Public Works. His mother was Anne Elizabeth, daughter of the late Hon. James Baby, at one time Speaker of the Legislative Council of Upper Canada. The subject of our sketch received a classical education at the College of Ste. Anne's, Quebec, afterwards taking a complete medical course at McGill University, Montreal, where he graduated in 1851 as Master of Surgery and Doctor of Medicine. In the course of the same year he began the practice of his profession in Detroit, where he remained until 1856, when, at the request of the people of Sandwich and Windsor, he removed to the latter place and took up his permanent residence. Shortly afterwards he was appointed Coroner and Jail Surgeon for the County of Essex. During all these years Mr. Casgrain has lived an energetic and useful life, and in every way has proved himself a good citizen. On the formation of the Essex Battalion in 1860, he was gazetted Captain of the Sandwich Company, and subsequently was surgeon to the troops at Windsor, during the Fenian raids of 1861-64. He served for three years as a Member of the Municipal Council, and for the period of eighteen years he was a Member of the Board of Education. He was elected first President of the St. Jean Baptiste Society of Essex in 1864, and has always taken an active interest in its welfare and success. In 1883 he held the office of general president of all the French Canadian societies in the County, and as such presided at the great Convention held under their auspices in Windsor during that year. Politically, Mr. Casgrain is a Conservative, and for many years has taken an active share in political contests, but, though often urged to place himself in the field as a candidate for political honours, he was obliged to decline, owing to the pressure of his professional duties. On January 12, 1887, he was called to the Senate, being the first French Canadian Senator from the Province of Ontario. In 1883, he was created a Knight of the Order of the Holy Sepulchre. He has been twice married: first, in 1851, to Charlotte Mary Chase, daughter of Thomas Chase, of Detroit, Michigan, formerly of Quebec; second, to Mary Ann Dougall, daughter of R. P. Street, formerly of Hamilton, Ont., now residing at Highland Park, Illinois.— *Windsor, Ont.*

HON. RAOUL DANDURAND.
(DeLorimier Division.)

The Hon. Raoul Dandurand was born in Montreal, November 4, 1861, his father being the late Œdipe Dandurand, merchant there, and was educated at the Montreal College. He received his legal training in the office of his cousin, the late Joseph Doutre, Q.C. In his practice at the Bar, Mr. Dandurand early attained an enviable position, and at the present time is head of the well-known firm of Dandurand, Brodeur & Boyer. He has taken an active part in politics, and at the last four general elections was the chief organizer of the Liberal Party in the district of Montreal, a position which required great tact and energy. He has been President of the Club National, and in 1891, for services rendered France, was created a Knight of the Legion of Honor. In conjunction with Mr. Charles Lanctot, Senator Dandurand is author of a "Treatise on Criminal Law" and a "Manual for Justices of the Peace." In 1886, Mr. Dandurand married Miss Josephine Marchand, a daughter of the present Premier of the Province of Quebec. Madame Dandurand is an authoress of some repute, a laureate of the Royal Society and Vice-President of the National Council of Women. A Liberal.—*Montreal.*

HON. JOHN LOVITT.
(Yarmouth.)

The Hon. John Lovitt was born at Yarmouth, N.S., October 9, 1832, and is the eldest son of the late John W. Lovitt. He was educated at the Academy there. He married in January, 1860, Elizabeth, second daughter of the late Robert Guest. He is by occupation a master mariner and shipowner, and is also a director of the Bank of Yarmouth. He represented Yarmouth in the House of Assembly of Nova Scotia from 1874 to 1878. He held a seat in the House of Commons from 1887 until 1891. He was called to the Senate, March 29, 1897. A Liberal.—*Yarmouth, N.S.*

HON. D. FERGUSON, P.C.
(Queen's.)

The Hon. Donald Ferguson was born at East River, Lot 34, P.E.I. His grandparents came from Blair, in Athol, Perthshire, Scotland, in 1806. He was educated at the Public Schools and also by private tuition. He is by occupation a farmer. He has been a J.P. since 1871. He was Collector of Inland Revenue for Charlottetown in 1873. He was elected to the Provincial Legislature for Cardigan District by acclamation in 1878, and again in 1879, when he accepted a seat in the Sullivan Administration with the Department of Public Works. He became Commissioner of Public Lands and Provincial Secretary in 1880, and held those offices until 1890. He was elected for the Fort Augustus District in 1882, 1886, 1887 and 1890. He resigned from the Provincial Legislature and Government in 1891, and ran for Queen's County in the Commons, but was defeated. He accepted a seat in Sir Mackenzie Bowell's Cabinet in December, 1894, without portfolio, and was Minister of Agriculture in Jan., 1896, and also held a seat in Sir Charles Tupper's Cabinet until its resignation in July, 1896. He was called to the Senate, September, 1893. A Liberal-Conservative.—*Tulloch, near Charlottetown, P.E.I.*

HON. J. A. LOUGHEED.
(Calgary.)

The Hon. James Alexander Lougheed was born in Brampton, County of Peel, Ont., September 1, 1854, but resided in Toronto until 1882. He married in September, 1884, the eldest daughter of the late William Hardisty, Chief Factor of the Hon Hudson's Bay Company. He was appointed a Q.C. by the Dominion Government in 1889. He studied law in Toronto, and practised there for a short time, but in 1882, removed to the North-West and settled in Calgary, N.W.T., where he has since been engaged in active legal practice. Appointed to the Senate on December 10, 1889. A Liberal-Conservative —*Calgary, N.W.T.*

HON. A. C. P. R. LANDRY, K.C.G.G.

(Stadacona.)

The Hon. Auguste Charles Philippe Robert Landry, A.B., was born at Quebec, January 15, 1846. He is the son of the late Dr. J. E. Landry, of Quebec, and Caroline Lelièvre. He was educated at the Seminary of Quebec and at St. Ann's Agricultural College. He received the degree of B.A. at the Seminary of Quebec. He married, October 6, 1868, Wilhelmina, daughter of the late Etienne Couture, of St. Gervais. He is by occupation a gentleman farmer. He is Lieut.-Col. of the 61st Batt. of Montmagny and L'Islet, and A. D. C. to His Excellency the Governor-General. He is Mayor of Limoilou. He is President of the Council of Agriculture of Quebec. He is Knight Commander of the Order of St. Gregory the Great, and Knight Commander of the Military Order of the Holy Sepulchre. He is a member of the Bibliographical Society of Paris. He was one of the Commissioners of the Province of Quebec to the Chicago Exhibition. He was first elected to the Quebec Legislative Assembly, for the County of Montmagny, at the general elections of 1875. He was elected to the Commons at the general elections of 1878 and 1882. Was called to the Senate, February 23, 1892. A Conservative.—*Mastai, Q.*

HON. J. D. LEWIN.

(St. John.)

The Hon. James Davies Lewin was born at Womaston, Radnorshire, April 1, 1812, and is a descendent of the Lewins of the same place. He was educated at the Kingston Grammar School, Wales. He was married in 1832 to Sarah Ann, daughter of the late Sherriff Clarke, New Brunswick, who was a United Empire Loyalist. He entered the employ of the British Government and was in their service when he came to New Brunswick in 1830 and continued in the office for twenty years. In 1855 he was elected to the Presidency of the Bank of New Brunswick, and still holds that position. He was appointed to the Senate, November 10, 1876. A Liberal.—*St. John, N.B.*

HON. L. F. R. MASSON,

(Mille Isles.)

The Hon. Louis Francois Rodrique Masson was born at Terrebonne, Que., November 7, 1833, and is the son of the late Hon. J. Masson. He was educated at Georgetown and Worcester, Mass., and at St. Hyacinthe College, Quebec. He married, first, in 1856, Louise Rachel, eldest daughter of the late Lieut.-Col. A. Mackenzie, and, second, in 1883, Cecile, daughter of Mr. J. H. Burroughs, Prothonotary, of Quebec. He was called to the Bar of Lower Canada in 1859. From 1863 to 1868 he was Brigade Major of the 8th Military District of Lower Canada and served during the Fenian Raids, and was promoted Lieut.-Col. in 1867. He was sworn of the Privy Council, as Minister of Militia and Defence, in October, 1878, and resigned in January, 1880, and accepted the portfolio of President of the Council, but resigned in November, 1880, on account of ill health. He held a seat in the Commons for Terrebonne from 1867 to 1882, when he was appointed to the Senate. He was Lieut.-Governor of the Province of Quebec from November, 1884, to October, 1887, when he resigned. In February, 1890, he was again appointed to the Senate. A Conservative.—*Terrebonne Q.*

HON W. OWENS, J P.

(Inkerman.)

The Hon. William Owens was born at Stonefield, County of Argenteuil, May 15, 1840, and is the son of Owen Owens, of Denbigh, Wales, and Charlotte Lindley, of Brantford, Eng. Mr. Owens was a Lieut. in the Active Militia, and has been Mayor, Councillor and Postmaster of the Township of Chatham. He was married in September, 1890, to Margaret, second daughter of Mr. J. Martin, of Chicago, who was previously a resident of Montreal. He held a seat in the Legislative Assembly of Quebec from the general elections, 1881, until 1891. when he resigned. He was appointed to the Senate, January 2, 1896. A Conservative.—*Montreal.*

HON. D. MacINNES.

(Burlington.)

The Hon. Donald MacInnes was born at Oban, Argyleshire, Scotland, on May 26, 1824, and came to Canada in 1840. He was married on April 30, 1863, to Mary Amelia, fourth daughter of the late Hon. Sir J. B. Robinson, Bart. Was for several years one of the leading merchants in Canada. Has been President of the Bank of Hamilton and of the Canada Cotton Co. of Cornwall, and also of the South Saskatchewan Valley Railway Co., and also a Director of the Canada Life Assurance Co. He was Chairman of the Royal Commission appointed June 16, 1880, to enquire into the organization of the Civil Service of Canada. The recommendations for the reform of the Service contained in the report of the Commissioners were embodied in an Act of Parliament, and is the Act under which the Service is now administered. He was called to the Senate on December 24, 1881. A Liberal-Conservative.—*Hamilton, O.*

HON. W. J. MACDONALD.

(Victoria, B.C.)

The Hon. William John Macdonald was born in the County of Inverness, Scotland, November 29, 1832, and was educated there. He is the third son of Major Macdonald, of Valley, North Uist, and Glendale, Isle of Skye. He was married March 17, 1857, to Catherine, second daughter of Capt. J. M. Read, of the Hon. H. B. Co.'s Service. He was elected Mayor of the City of Victoria in 1866 and 1871. He was a Savings' Bank Commissioner, Public School Commissioner, Road Commissioner and has held various colonial appointments. He has been Collector of Customs in Vancouver Island, and was also a Captain of the Militia. Was a member of the Legislative Council and Assembly for two terms. He sat for Sooke in Vancouver Island Assembly for several years. Appointed to the Senate, December 13, 1871, one of the first Senators on British Columbia entering the Dominion. A Liberal-Conservative.—*Victoria, B.C.*

HON. J. R. GOWAN, C.M.G., LL.D., Q.C.

(Barrie.)

The Hon. James Robert Gowan, son of Henry Hatton Gowan, was born at Cahore, Co. Wexford, Ireland, Dec. 22, 1815. The family is Milesian, tracing descent from one of the Red Branch Knights of Ulster. He married in 1854, Anne, daughter of Rev. S. B. Ardagh, A. M. In 1843 appointed Judge. 1869, Chairman of the Board of Judges for Ontario; retired from Judicial office 1883. *General services :* From 1843 to 1893, on G. S. and Collegiate Institute Board; from 1844 to 1871, Chairman Board of Public Instruction; 1857, Associate in framing tariff of fees for profession and officers of the Courts; 1858, one of three Judges framing rules under law assimilating Probate and Administration to that of England; 1862, Judicial Umpire on differences between the Government and contractors touching erection of Parliamentary Buildings at Ottawa; 1873, on Royal Commission of Judges to enquire into charges against Cabinet Ministers, in connection with C.P.R. contracts; 1871, on Government Commission as to "fusing law and equity." Engaged in various consolidations of the Statute law, and 1868 and 1869 consolidation of the Statute law of Upper Canada (from 1792) and of Canada; 1869, of Criminal Law Statutes; 1879, of the Statutes of Ontario, and 1892 co-operated in the work of the Criminal Code. For more than 30 years, at the instance of law officers of the Crown, under successive Governments, rendered voluntary service in Parliamentary and other drafting. In 1885 appointed a Senator, and is now a member. For ten sessions was Chairman of the Special Committee on Divorce in the Senate. Created a C. M. G. in 1893, "on recognition of his valuable services in Canada."—*Ardraven, Barrie, O.*

HON. L. G. POWER, LL.B.

(Halifax)

The Hon. Lawrence Geoffrey Power was born at Halifax, N.S., August 9, 1841. He was educated at St. Mary's College, Halifax, Carlow College, The Catholic University, Ireland, and Harvard Law School, Cambridge, Mass., where he received the degree of LL.B. in 1866. Was married June 23, 1880, to Susan, daughter of Mr. M. O'Leary, of West Quoddy. He was admitted to the Bar in 1866. He was an alderman of the City of Halifax for six years, and was a member of the Board of School Commissioners for thirteen years. Is a member of the Senate of the University of Halifax. He was actively engaged in the preparation of the Revised Statutes of Nova Scotia, 4th Series, 1874, and Laws and Ordinances relating to the City of Halifax, 1876. Is the author of a pamphlet, "The Manitoba School Question, from the point of view of a Catholic Member," and has been an occasional contributor to magazines and a frequent one to newspapers. He was called to the Senate February 2, 1877. A Reformer.—*Halifax, N.S.*

HON. W. MILLER, Q.C., P.C.

(Richmond.)

The Hon. William Miller was born at Antigonish, N. S., February 12, 1834, and is the son of Charles Miller of Antigonish, N.S. Was educated at St. Andrew's Grammar School and Antigonish Academy. He married in October, 1871, Anne, daughter of the late Hon. James Cochrane, of Halifax, N.S. He was called to the Bar of N.S. in 1860, and was appointed Q.C. in 1872. He sat in the N.S. Assembly from 1863 until the time of the Union. Mr. Miller has been chairman of the Select Joint Committee of both Houses on the codification of the Criminal Laws which reported the present Criminal Code. He was appointed to the Senate by Royal Proclamation in 1867, and was Speaker from 1883 to 1887. In 1891 he was appointed a member of the Queen's Privy Council for Canada. A Conservative.—*Arichat, N.S.*

HON. LIEUT.-COL. A. W. OGILVIE, J.P.

(Alma.)

The Hon. Alexander Walker Ogilvie was born at Cote St. Michel, Que., May 7, 1829. He is of Scotch descent, his parents having come to Canada in 1800, his father serving in the War of 1812, and also as a Volunteer Cavalry Officer during the Rebellion in 1837. He was educated in Montreal. He was married to Sarah, daughter of William Leney, Esq. Founded the firm of A. W. Ogilvie & Co., proprietors of the Glenora Mills, Montreal, in 1854. Is on the retired list as Lieut.-Col. of Montreal Cavalry. He is Past president of St. Andrew's Society, the Widows and Orphans Benevolent Society, and the Montreal Turnpike Trust. He is President of the Western Loan & Trust Co., President of the St. Michel Road Company, Vice-President of the Sun Life Insurance Co., the Montreal Loan & Mortgage Co., and the Dominion Burglary Co. Has been a member of the City Councils of Montreal and Quebec. Sat in the Quebec Legislative Assembly from 1867 until 1871, in which year he declined renomination. Was re-elected in 1875 and sat until 1878, in which year he resigned. Called to the Senate, December, 1881.—A Conservative.—*Montreal.*

HON. E. J. PRICE, D.C.L.

(Laurentides.)

The Hon. Evan John Price was born at Wolfesfield, in the vicinity of Quebec, May 8, 1840. He is the fourth son of the late William Price, a lumber merchant of Quebec and the Saguenay, and Jane, third daughter of the late Charles Stewart, Esq., who was Comptroller of the Imperial Customs at Quebec, and grandson of Richard Price, Esq., of Elstree, Herts, Eng. He was educated in England. Mr. Price is the only surviving partner in the lumbering, manufacturing and exporting company of Price Brothers, of Quebec and the Saguenay. He is a director of several commercial companies, and is Vice-President of the Union Bank of Canada. Appointed to the Senate, December 1, 1888. A Conservative.—*Quebec.*

HON. JAMES O'BRIEN.
(Victoria.)

The Hon. James O'Brien was born at Aughnagar, County of Tyrone, Ireland, August 3, 1836. He was educated there. He removed to Canada in 1850, and in 1858 he started business in the wholesale clothing and dry goods trade in Montreal. He retired from that business in 1893. He is a director of the City and District Savings Bank, The Royal Victoria Life Insurance Company, also a member of the Board of Trade. He is a Life Governor of the Montreal General Hospital, of the Western and Notre Dame Hospitals, and is also a trustee of St. Patrick's Orphan Asylum, and is a Governor of Laval University. He was one of the founders of the Dominion Commercial Travellers' Association. Appointed to the Senate, January 2, 1896. A Liberal-Conservative.—*Montreal.*

HON. JOHN O'DONOHOE, Q.C.
(Erie.)

The Hon. John O'Donohoe was born at Tuam, Galway, April 18, 1824. He was educated at St. Jarlath's College, of the same place. In 1839 he emigrated to Toronto, where he now resides. He married, in 1848, Charlotte Josephine, daughter of Dr. Bradley of Toronto. He was called to the Bar of Ontario in 1869, and was appointed Q.C. in 1880. He was Secretary of St. Patrick's Benevolent Society at the time the late Hon. Robert Baldwin was President, and was President for several years after Mr. Baldwin's resignation. He is a Captain in the Militia. In April, 1871, he was elected President of the "Ontario Catholic League." At the general elections of 1871 and 1872 he was defeated for East Peterboro in the Ontario Assembly, and for Toronto East in the House of Commons. He was first elected to the House for Toronto East in 1874, but was unseated on petition in November, 1874, and was again defeated. He was appointed to the Senate in May, 1872. A Liberal.—*Toronto, O.*

HON. A. A. MACDONALD.
(Charlottetown.)

The Hon. Andrew Archibald Macdonald was born at Three Rivers, P.E.I., February 14, 1829. He was educated at the County Grammar School and also by a private tutor. He was married in 1863 to Elizabeth, daughter of the late Thos. Owen, formerly Provincial Postmaster-General. He held a seat in the House of Assembly from 1854 to 1860. In 1863, when the Legislative became elective, he was elected for King's County, 2nd District, in Legislative Council, and was re-elected in 1867. He continued to sit in that body until 1873, when he received the appointment of Postmaster-General of the Province. He was a delegate to the Charlottetown Conference on the Union of the Lower Provinces in 1864, and was also a delegate to the Quebec Conference in the same year, and to the International Convention at Portland, Me., U.S.A., in 1868. He was a member of the Board of Education from 1867 until 1870. He was leader of the Government Party in the Legislative Council for several years, and was Lieut.-Governor of Prince Edward Island from 1884 to 1889. He was appointed to the Senate, May 11, 1891. A Liberal-Conservative.—*Charlottetown, P.E.I.*

HON. D. McMILLAN, M.D.
(Alexandria.)

The Hon. Donald McMillan was born in Glengarry, Ont., March 5, 1835. He was educated there and also by private tuition. In 1855 he received the degree of M.D. at the Victoria University of Toronto. He was married November 17, 1857, to Amy Ann, daughter of Amasa Lewis, Esq., J.P., of Aylmer, Ont. He has held various public offices, such as Vice-President of the Medical Association of Ontario, and for several years was a member of the County Council. He is now a J. P. and an Associate Coroner for Glengarry, and is also an honorary member of the Celtic Society of Montreal. He was appointed to the Senate on January 11 1884. A Conservative.—*Alexandria, O.*

HON. J. N. KIRCHHOFFER.
(Selkirk.)

The Hon. John Nesbitt Kirchhoffer was born in Ballyromney Parish, Co. Cork, Ireland, on May 5, 1848. His greatgrandfather, a member of a Swiss family, was surgeon to William, Prince of Orange, with whom he went to Ireland, and was present at the battle of the Boyne, where he extracted from the Monarch's arm a bullet, which is still preserved as an heirloom in the family. He is a son of the Reverend Richard B. Kirchhoffer, Rector of Ballyromney Parish, Co. Cork, Ireland. He was educated at Marlborough College, one of the great English Public Schools, and came to Canada in 1864. Took part in the Fenian Raid troubles in 1866, being Ensign and subsequently Captain of one of the Companies of the Port Hope (46th) Batt. Called to the Bar Oct., 1871, and practiced law in Port Hope with his uncle, the late Nesbitt Kirchhoffer, Q.C. Married, first, Ada, daughter of the late Dr. Wm. Smith, of Port Hope, and second, Clara, daughter of the late Rev. J. B. Howard, a lady of well-known literary and artistic abilities as well as great personal attractions. Moved to Manitoba in 1883, and was called to the Bar there in 1884. Founded and successfully completed the Punn Creek Settlement, now one of the most thriving parts of the prairie province. Was successively Reeve and Mayor of Souris, and a member of the Western Judicial Board, of which he subsequently became Chairman. Sat in the Legislative Assembly of Manitoba from 1886 to 1888. Called to the Senate December 16, 1892. Was Chairman of the Senate Divorce Committee in 1895 and 1896, and of the Senate Contingent Committee in 1897. A Conservative.—*Brandon, Man.*

HON. SAMUEL MERNER.
(Hamburg.)

The Hon. Samuel Merner was born in Reichenboch, Canton of Berne, Switzerland, January 29, 1823. He is the son of Jacob Merner, a farmer of the same place. He was educated at Reichenboch, and removed to Canada with his parents in 1837. For several years he did business as an iron founder and manufacturer of furniture. He was married to Mary Anne, daughter of Joseph Grasser, of Wilmot, Ont. He has been Reeve of New Hamburg for several years, and was Warden of Waterloo County in 1873. He has been engaged for several years in the settling in the Province of all the Swiss people emigrating to Canada. At a by-election held in 1877, he was an unsuccessful candidate in the Legislative Assembly for South Waterloo. He held a seat for the same constituency in the Commons from 1878, when he defeated the Hon. James Young, of Galt, to 1882, when he was defeated. He was appointed to the Senate, January 12, 1887. A Conservative.—*New Hamburg, O.*

HON. P. POIRIER, M.A.
(Acadie.)

The Hon. Pascal Poirier was born at Shediac, N.B., February, 15, 1852. He was educated at the St. Joseph College, Memramcook, N.B. He was married in 1879 to Anna Lusignan. He was Postmaster of the House of Commons from 1872 to 1885. Was President of a section of the French Canadian Institute, Ottawa, in 1882 and 1883, and was also President of the Mineralogical Society of Ottawa University. He is a barrister of both New Brunswick and the Province of Quebec. Mr. Poirier is the author of " L'Origine des Acadiens," and of various contributions in newspapers and reviews. He is now President of " La Société de l'Assomption " for the Maritime Provinces. Was appointed to the Senate March 9, 1885. A Liberal-Conservative.—*Shediac, N. B.*

HON. SIR W. H. HINGSTON, K.B., M.D., LL.D., D.C.L.
(Rougemont.)

The Hon. Sir William Hales Hingston was born at Hinchinbrook, County of Huntingdon, P. Q., June 29, 1829. He is the son of the late Lieut.-Col. Hingston, formerly of H. M. 100th Regiment, who afterwards commanded the Militia of the District of Beauharnois. He was educated at the Montreal College and studied medicine at McGill University, graduating at the latter in 1851. He then studied in Edinburgh, where he took his surgeon's diploma as L.R.C.S.E. He subsequently received diplomas from the highest scientific bodies in Austria, Prussia, Bavaria, France, England and the United States. He is D.C.L. of Lennoxville University, and LL.D. of Victoria University. He began practice in Montreal in 1853, devoting his time chiefly to surgery. He has held the offices of President of the Canadian Medical Association, of the College of Physicians and Surgeons of the Province of Quebec, several times of the Medico-Chirurgical Society of Montreal, and has been Vice-President of the British Association for the Advancement of Science. He was Mayor of Montreal during 1876 and 1877, having been elected the first time by a majority of ten to one, and the second time unanimously. During his Mayoralty he organized the Local and Provincial Boards of Health which have since done so much service. He has long been a Director and is now President of the Montreal City and District Savings Bank. He was married in 1875 to Margaret Josephine, daughter of the late Hon. D. A. Macdonald, then Lieut.-Governor of Ontario. He was knighted by Her Majesty in May, 1895, for distinguished services to Medical Science, and was appointed to the Senate, January 2, 1896. A Liberal-Conservative.—*Montreal*.

HON. DAVID REESOR.
(King's.)

The Hon. David Reesor was born in the Township of Markham, Ont., January 18, 1823, and is of German descent. He was educated in Markham. Mr. Reesor was the founder of the Markham *Economist*, and was for several years the editor of that paper. He was married to Emily, eldest daughter of the late D. McDougall, Esq., of St. Mary's, Ont., and a sister of the Hon. W. McDougall, C.B. He was elected to the Legislative Council for King's from 1860, which seat he held until the time of the Union, when he was appointed to the Senate for life. He has also been Warden of the Counties of York and Peel. He was appointed to the Senate by Royal Proclamation in May, 1867. A Liberal.—*Yorkville, O.*

HON. M. SULLIVAN, M.D.
(Kingston.)

The Hon. Michael Sullivan was born at Killarney, County of Kerry, Ireland, February 13, 1838. Came to Canada in 1842, and now resides in Kingston. Was educated at the Regiopolis College and received the degree of M.D. in 1858, at Queen's College. He married in June, 1867, Mary Brown of Kingston. He served as Purveyor-General during the Northwest Rebellion of 1885. In 1872 he was appointed Lecturer in Anatomy in Queen's College, and at the time of the establishment of the Royal College of Surgeons and Physicians in affiliation with Queen's University, he was appointed Professor of Anatomy. In 1883 he was President of the Medical Association of Canada, and has also been Alderman and Mayor of Kingston. He is now a Professor of Surgery and Histology, and is a trustee of the Kingston Hospital and a member of the Ontario Medical Association. He ran for the Commons in 1882 for Kingston, but was defeated. He was appointed to the Senate in January, 1885. A Conservative.—*Kingston, O.*

HON. THOMAS McKAY.
(Truro.)

The Hon. Thomas McKay was born in Pictou County, N. S., January 8, 1839. He is of Scotch descent, and is the son of the late William McKay, who emigrated from Sutherlandshire, Scotland, and settled in the County of Pictou, N. S. He was educated in Pictou. Married in November, 1868, Jessie fourth daughter of the late John Blair, of Truro. By occupation a merchant. First elected to the House of Commons for Colchester, at the general elections held in 1874; was unseated on petition in November of the same year. He was re-elected, and sat from December, 1874, to May, 1881. He was called to the Senate, December 24, 1881. A Liberal-Conservative.—*Truro, N. S.*

HON. WILLIAM McDONALD.
(Cape Breton.)

The Hon. William McDonald was born at the Settlement of River Deny's Road, Inverness County, N.S., October 7, 1837, and is of Scottish descent. His father, Allan McDonald, who emigrated from South Uist, Inverness-shire, Scotland, in the early part of the century, settled as a farmer at River Deny's. His mother was Mary, daughter of William McDonald, of Stollegarry, Barra, Scotland, and still living in her 92nd year. He was educated at St. Francois Xavier College, Antigonish, N.S. In 1864 he engaged in commercial pursuits, in which he was successful. He always took an interest in public matters, and held Municipal, Provincial and Federal offices. He was first elected to the House of Commons in 1872. He held the confidence of the people in a marvellous degree. He was for several years Chairman of the Committee on Immigration and Colonization. In 1884 he was called to the Senate; he is moderate in his political opinions and deprecates extremes. Mr. McDonald was married in 1865 to Catherine, daughter of the late Donald McDonald, Sydney Forks, by whom he has a family of three sons and three daughters.—*Little Glace Bay, N.S.*

HON. G. C. McKINDSEY.
(Milton.)

The Hon. George Crawford McKindsey was born in the Township of Trafalgar, County of Halton, March 29, 1829. He is of Irish descent, and his parents, who were both natives of the North of Ireland, came to Canada and settled in the County of Halton in 1819. He was educated at the Common School and also by private tuition. He married in October, 1859, Teresa Crawford. He has held several public offices, such as Deputy Sheriff, from July, 1855, until October, 1858, and that of Sheriff of the County of Halton from October, 1858, until June, 1882; also President of the Agricultural Association of Halton County. He has been a Captain in the Militia and a J. P. He was appointed to the Senate in January, 1884. A Conservative.—*Milton, O.*

HON. C. PRIMROSE.
(Pictou.)

The Hon. Clarence Primrose was born at Pictou, October 5, 1830. He is the son of the late James Primrose, of Pictou, Nova Scotia, a banker and merchant, and whose father was the Rev. John Primrose, of the Parish of "Grange", Banffshire, Scotland. He was educated at the Pictou Academy and also at the High School and University of Edinburgh, Scotland. He married, June 28, 1858, at Pictou, Rachel Carré, daughter of the late Henry Carré, Esq., merchant, formerly of Guernsey, Channel Islands. Is the senior partner of the firm of Primrose Brothers, of Pictou, N.S., insurance, lumber and general commission merchants. He has been President of the Young Men's Christian Association of Pictou; of the Pictou Marine Railway Company; the Maritime Marine Insurance Company; the Pictou Publishing Company, and also of the Liberal-Conservative Central Executive Committee. He was appointed to the Senate, November 28, 1892. A Liberal-Conservative.—*Pictou, N.S.*

HON. PETER McLAREN.
(Perth.)

The Hon. Peter McLaren was born at Lanark, Ont., September 21, 1833. He comes of loyal British stock. Is a son of James McLaren who came from Perthshire, Scotland, in 1820, and settled in Lanark, Ont. Was a lieutenant in the Militia when the trouble arose in 1837 between the United States and Canada. His grandfather, Peter McLaren, belonged to Lochiel's Highland Regiment, and was engaged in the Irish rebellion of 1815 He also fought in Spain. Mr. McLaren was for years engaged in the manufacture of sawn lumber and timber, and still retains large lumbering interests in the North West. He is also interested in large timber areas and iron lands in Virginia. He is married to Sophia, daughter of William Lees, and granddaughter of the late Col. Playfair. This well-known officer marched afoot with his command from New Brunswick to Quebec through a wilderness with from four to six feet of snow on the ground, and arrived without the loss of a man. Col. Playfair while a member of the old Parliament of Canada, took an active part in bringing about the selection of Ottawa as the Capital of Canada, and was the first person known to have advocated the construction of a Canadian Pacific Railway, having written on the subject to the London press in the early fifties in a pamphlet on Colonial defence. - *Perth, O.*

HON. H. MONTPLAISIR.
(Shawenegan)

The Hon. Hypolite Montplaisir was borne at Cap de la Madeleine, Province of Quebec, March 7, 1840, and is the son of Mr. Paschal Montplaisir and Victoire Crevier. He was educated at Three Rivers. Mr. Montplaisir is extensively engaged in farming. He has held several important offices such as Mayor of the Parish and Warden of the county for several years and Secretary Treasurer of the Schools. He was first elected to the House of Commons for Champlain at the general elections held in 1874, and sat until the close of the Sixth Parliament in 1891. Appointed to the Senate, Feb. 9, 1891. A Liberal-Conservative.—*Cap de la Madeleine, Q.*

HON. SAMUEL PROWSE.
(King's, P.E.I.)

The Hon. Samuel Prowse was born in the Royalty of Charlottetown, August 28, 1835, and was educated at the same place. Is the son of the late Mr. William Prowse, who removed from Devonshire, England, to Prince Edward Island in 1823. Was a member of the Executive Council from 1876, until 1878, and was reappointed in 1879. Was first elected to the House of Assembly at the general election in 1867 for King's, 4th District. In 1876 he was re-elected for the same seat, and accepted a seat in the Coalition Government on the School Question. Resigned his seat in the Government in 1878, was re-elected in 1879, and accepted a seat in the Liberal-Conservative Government. Was re-elected in 1882 and also in 1886. He sat in the House of Assembly until 1889. Called to the Senate September, 1889. A Liberal-Conservative.—*Murray Harbour, P.E.I.*

HON. DAVID MacKEEN.
(Cape Breton.)

The Hon. David MacKeen was born at Mabou, Nova Scotia, September 20, 1839. His ancestors emigrated to Canada from Ireland and Scotland, and he is the son of the late Hon. William MacKeen, M.L.C., Nova Scotia. He was Treasurer and Agent of the Caledonia Coal and Railway Company, also Resident Manager of the Dominion Coal Co. during the first years of its operations in Cape Breton. In 1867 he married, Crst, Isabel, daughter of the late Mr. Henry Poole, of Derby, England, and, second, in 1877, Frances M., daughter of the late William Lawson, Esq., of Halifax; third, in 1888, Janie K., daughter of the late John Crerar, Esq., of Halifax. Mr MacKeen has held several public offices, such as U. S. Consular Agent, Sub-Collector of Customs, Municipal Councillor and Warden of Cape Breton County. He was first elected to the House of Commons in 1887, and was re-elected in 1891, and held his seat until his resignation in January, 1896. Appointed to the Senate, Feb. 21, 1896. A Conservative.—*Caledonia Mines, Little Glace Bay, N.S.*

HON. JOSIAH WOOD.
(Westmoreland.)

The Hon. Josiah Wood, M.A., was born on April 18, 1843, in Sackville, N.B., being the son of Mariner Wood, a merchant of Sackville, N.B. He was educated at Mount Allison Wesleyan College, Sackville, where he graduated in 1863, and in 1866 he received the degree of M.A. He married on January 14, 1874, Laura S., daughter of Thompson Trueman, of Sackville. He was called to the Bar of New Brunswick in 1866. After following that profession for a short time, he entered his father's business, of which firm he is now the only surviving partner. He is largely interested in farming and stock-raising, and is also a shipowner. He is Treasurer of the Board of Regents of Mount Allison College. He unsuccessfully contested Westmoreland for the Legislative Assembly of N.B. at the general election held in 1878. He was first elected to Parliament at the general election held in 1882, and was re-elected at the general elections of 1887 and 1891. He resigned, and was called to the Senate on August 5, 1895. A Conservative.—*Sackville, N.B.*

HON. JOSEPH R. THIBAUDEAU.
(Rigaud.)

The Hon. Joseph Rosaire Thibaudeau was born at Cap Santé, County of Portneuf, October 1, 1837. He is a descendant of a French family which existed in the reign of Louis XV, and upon the breaking out of the French Revolution in 1789, removed to Acadia, and subsequently to Lower Canada. He was married December 9, 1873, to Marguerite LaMothe, the eldest daughter of Guillaume LaMothe, Esq., formerly Postmaster of Montreal. He holds the offices of President of the Royal Electric Company, President of the Atlantic and Lake Superior Railway Company, Chairman of the Alliance Assurance Company of London, England, Vice-President of the Montreal Park and Island Railway Company, Director of Notre Dame Hospital, etc. He was appointed Sheriff of Montreal, May 9, 1890. Called to the Senate in January, 1878. A Liberal.—*Montreal.*

HON. THOMAS TEMPLE.
(York, N. B.)

The Hon. Thomas Temple, Senator for York, N. B., ex-M. P. and ex-Sheriff of the same County, was born at Bampton, Oxfordshire, England, on November 4, 1818. He is a son of Charles Temple, who came to this country in 1832. His father adopted the usual occupation of the time, farming, and the son helped him. At the age of twenty he obtained a gift horse from his father, and joined a Company of York Light Dragoons under Major Wilmot, this Corps having been raised "to protect the interests of the Province during the troubles which existed between the Colonies and the United States in regard to the boundary line between the Province of New Brunswick and the bordering State of Maine." It was after this that Mr. Temple, having good foresight, at once perceived that the lumbering business offered an excellent field for enterprise, and embarking in this business he soon had achieved so much success that he was enabled to purchase the splendid Poquiock Mills. He is now engaged in the lumber business on an extensive scale There is no other man to whom the central portion of New Brunswick is as much indebted as Mr. Temple. In 1869, in conjunction with Mr. Burpee, he began the construction of what is known as the Fredericton Branch Railway, a road which gave the Capital and the country surrounding it connection with the Western Extension Railway (formerly the St. John and Maine Railway), which connects with the great railway system. In 1871 it was completed and ready for traffic, and Mr. Temple has remained its President since. Mr. Temple is proprietor of the largest farm in New Brunswick, situated in Gloucester County, it having an area of five hundred and thirty acres. For about twenty years Mr. Temple held the position of Sheriff of York. He is a director of the People's Bank of Fredericton. Upon the death of John Pickard, in 1884, he contested York in the interests of the Conservative party, and was successful, defeating his opponent by 178 votes. In 1887 he was again re-elected over Mr. Gregory by a majority of four hundred, and again in 1891 he defeated the Hon. F. P. Thompson by a majority of two hundred and twenty-seven. He retained his seat until the month of April, 1896, when he was called to the Senate. Mr. Temple has made a valuable representative, for among the many benefits conferred upon his constituency the greatest was his splendid achievement of bridging the St. John between Fredericton and St. Mary's. The Canada Eastern Railway, which otherwise could not reach Fredericton, attains its entrance over this bridge. Mr. Temple married in October, 1840, Susanna, only daughter of Solomon Howe, of Maine, and has by this lady five children.—*Fredericton, N.B.*

HON. JAMES REID.
(Cariboo.)

The Hon. James Reid was born in the Township of Hull, August 2, 1839, is of Irish descent, and is the third son of James and Anna Reid, who in 1832 removed from the North of Ireland and came to Canada, settling in the Township of Hull, P.Q. He was educated in the common schools. Was married February 14, 1883, to Charlotte, youngest daughter of Nicholas Clarke, of Manotic, Ont. He proceeded to British Columbia in 1862, and is now extensively engaged in mercantile and mining pursuits, and is owner of the Cariboo Flour and Lumber Mills and manager of the North British Columbia Navigation Co.'s boats in the Cariboo District; also President of the Quesnelle Quartz Mining Co., Cariboo, and also of the Blue Lead Hydraulic Mining Co. He was first elected to the House of Commons for Cariboo in March, 1881, and continued to sit until October, 1888. He was called to the Senate in 1888. A Liberal-Conservative.—*Quesnelle, B.C.*

HON. T. ROBITAILLE, M.D., P.C.
(Gulf.)

The Hon. Theodore Robitaille was born at Varennes, P. Q., January 29, 1834, and died August 17, 1897. He was the son of the late Louis Adolphe Robitaille, N.P. He was educated at the Model School, at the Seminary of St. Therese, at Laval University and at the McGill College, Montreal, where he received the degree of M.D. in 1858. He married in November, 1867, Marie Josephine Charlotte Emma, daughter of P. A. Quesnel, Esq. He held a seat in the Assembly for Bonaventure from 1861 until the Union, and from 1867 until 1879 he sat in the Commons for the same constituency. He was sworn of the Privy Council, and was Receiver-General from January, 1873, to November of the same year, when he resigned with Sir John A. Macdonald. He was Lieut.-Governor of Quebec from July, 1879, to November, 1884. He was appointed to the Senate in January, 1885. Was a Conservative.

HON. J. J. ROSS, M.D.
(De la Durantaye.)

The Hon. John Jones Ross was born at Quebec, August 16, 1833, and is the son of G. McIntosh Ross, Esq., of St. Anne's. He married in 1856 Marie Arline, daughter of Lieut.-Col. Lanouette, of Champlain. He is President of the Provincial College of Physicians and Surgeons, and Honorary President of the Champlain Agricultural Society. From July, 1881, until March, 1882, he was Commissioner of Agriculture and Public Works, when he resigned from the Cabinet. In January, 1884, upon the resignation of the Mousseau Ministry, he formed an Administration, and became Premier and Commissioner of Agriculture and Public Works, but resigned with his colleagues in 1887. Sat for Champlain in Canadian Assembly from g. e., 1861, until the Union, when returned to Commons and Legislative Assembly. Resigned his seat in the latter on his appointment to Legislative Council, Quebec, 1867. He was appointed to the Senate in April, 1887, and was Speaker of that House from September, 1891, until April, 1896. He was sworn of the Privy Council and a member of Sir Charles Tupper's Ministry from May until July, 1896, when he resigned with his colleagues. A Conservative.—*Ste. Anne de la Perade, Que.*

HON. J. SUTHERLAND.
(Kildonan.)

The Hon. John Sutherland was born in Winnipeg, August 23, 1821. He is the son of Mr. A. Sutherland, of Sutherlandshire, Scotland, who served in the British Army in the Peninsula Campaign, and who came to Canada and settled in the city of Winnipeg in 1815. He was educated at St. John's College. He married the second daughter of Mr. John Macbeth, of Winnipeg. Mr. Sutherland was a member of the Council of Assiniboia from 1866 until its abolition. He was a director of the Commercial Bank, Manitoba, and of the Winnipeg Trusts Company. In 1870 he was High Sheriff of Manitoba. He reisgned that office upon being appointed to the Senate in 1871. An Independent Conservative.—*Kildonan, Man.*

HON. SIR F. SMITH, KNT.

(Toronto.)

The Hon. Sir Frank Smith was born at Richhill, Armagh, Ireland, in 1822, and came to Canada with his father in 1832, settling in the vicinity of Toronto. He married a daughter of Mr. J. O'Higgins, J. P., of Stratford, in 1852. In 1866 he was elected Mayor of London. He has held several public offices such as President of Northern and North Western Railway, Toronto Street Ry. Co., London and Ontario Investment Co., Ontario Jockey Club, Niagara Navigation Co., and is now President of the Dominion Bank and Home Savings & Loan Co., Vice President of Dominion Telegraph Co. and Consumers Gas Co., Director of North American Life Assurance Co. and Toronto General Trusts Co. He was appointed to the Senate in February, 1871, and served in the Ministry about 18 years : first in the Cabinet of Sir John A. Macdonald about 1878 ; then he was Minister of Public Works in the Abbott Ministry from 1891 to January, 1892, and without portfolio until November, 1892 ; was also a member of the Thompson and Bowell Administrations, and then became a member of Sir Charles Tupper's Ministry, without porfolio. He was created a Knight Bachelor in June, 1894. He resigned with his colleagues in July, 1896.—*Toronto, Ont.*

HON. W. TEMPLEMAN.

(Victoria City, B.C.)

Hon. William Templeman was born at Pakenham, County of Lanark, Ont., in 1845, of Scottish parentage and descent. He was educated at the Public School, and afterwards became connected with the newspaper business. He established the Almonte *Gazette* in 1867, which he carried on successfully for some time. He migrated to Victoria, B.C., in 1884, and has since published the Victoria *Times*, a newspaper which has a large circulation in British Columbia and the North-West. He was appointed to the Senate in November, 1897.—*Victoria, B.C*

HON. A. A. THIBAUDEAU.

(De la Vallière.)

The Hon. Alfred A. Thibaudeau was born in Quebec, December 1, 1860. He is the son of the Hon. Isidore Thibaudeau, M. P. for Quebec from 1873 until 1878, and is of French descent. He was educated at the Quebec High School. He was married January 9, 1894, to Eva, daughter of the late Senator Rodier, of Montreal. He is in business as a merchant, and is head of the firm of Thibaudeau Brothers. He has held the office of President of the Wholesale Dry-Goods Association, and is a member of Council of the Montreal Board of Trade. He is a director of the Notre Dame Hospital, Governor of Laval University, and a director of the Great West Life Assurance Company, and of the Park & Island Railway Co. of Montreal. He was appointed to the Senate, August, 1896.—*Montreal.*

HON. LACHLAN McCALLUM.

(Monck.)

The Hon. Lachlan McCallum was born in the Island of Tiree, Argyleshire, Scotland, on March 15, 1823, and came to Canada in 1842. He married in October, 1854, Priscilla Dawson Thewlis. He is by occupation a contractor, shipbuilder and shipowner. For some years he was Reeve of the United Townships of Sherbrooke and Moulton. He was Captain of the Dunville Naval Company, which force he commanded at Fort Erie, at the time of the Fenian Raid, in June, 1866. He sat in the Commons from the general elections of 1867 until the general elections of 1872, when he was defeated. He sat from 1871 until 1872 in the Legislative Assembly of Ontario, when he resigned in consequence of the passing of the Act abolishing dual representation. He was re-elected to the House of Commons at the general elections of 1874, and was unseated on petition on May 12, 1875. He was re-elected June 22, 1875, and sat until the dissolution of that Parliament in 1887. Called to the Senate, February, 4, 1887. A Liberal-Conservative.—*Stromness, Ont.*

HON. J. B. SNOWBALL.

(Chatham, N.B.)

The Hon. Jabez Bunting Snowball was born at Lunenburg, N.S., Sept. 24, 1837, and is the son of Rev. John Snowball, a native of Yorkshire, England. He was educated at Mount Allison Wesleyan College, Sackville, N.B. He married first Margaret, daughter of John McDougall, Esq., and, second, on February 18, 1873, at Airdrie, Scotland, to Maggie E., daughter of the Rev. Robert Archibald of New Monkland, Scotland. He has been largely identified with Railway enterprises in New Brunswick, and connected with all important enterprises in Northumberland County, where he now resides. He is extensively engaged in the export timber trade, and is the owner of several steam saw mills and tug boats. He ran for the House of Commons in the Liberal interest in 1874, but was defeated, and in 1878 he ran again and defeated Mr. Mitchell. He sat in the Commons for Northumberland, N.B., from 1878 until 1882, when he resigned. Called to the Senate, May 1, 1891. An Independent.—*Chatham, N.B.*

HON. J. B. R. FISET, M.D.

(Rimouski.)

The Hon. Jean Bte. Romuald Fiset was born at St. Cuthbert, P.Q., Feb. 7, 1843, and is the son of the late Henri Fiset of St. Cuthbert. He was educated at the Montreal College and at Laval University at Quebec, where he graduated an M.D. in 1868. He married Aimée, daughter of the late Honoré Plamondon, of Quebec. He is a Governor of the College of Physicians and Surgeons of Quebec, and has been Councillor and subsequently Mayor of Rimouski. He was appointed Surgeon of the 89th Batt., Rimouski, in 1871, and in September, 1895, was elevated to the rank of Surgeon-Major. In 1872 he was elected to the Commons for Rimouski, and sat until 1882, when he was defeated. He was defeated in 1891, but re-elected at the general elections held in 1896. Called to the Senate October 20, 1897. A Liberal.—*Rimouski, Q.*

HON. W. E. SANFORD.

(Hamilton.)

The Hon. William Eli Sanford was born in the City of New York in 1838. His first wife was Emeline, only daughter of the late Edward Jackson, Esq., who died in 1860. In 1866 he married Harriet Sophia, daughter of the late Thomas Vaux, Esq., of Ottawa. He is President and Managing Director of The W. E. Sanford Manufacturing Company. He is also President of the Hamilton Ladies' College and is a member of the Board of Regents of Victoria University. In the past he has held the positions of President of the Hamilton Board of Trade, Vice-President of the Hamilton Provident and Loan Society, and Commodore of the Royal Hamilton Yacht Club. He was identified with the early history of Manitoba, and is at present time one of the largest land owners in that Province. He was a Director of the Portage and Westbourne Railway. Called to the Senate February 8, 1887. A Conservative.—*Hamilton, Ont.*

HON. J. O. VILLENEUVE.

(DeSalaberry.)

The Hon. Joseph Octave Villeneuve was born at Ste. Anne des Plaines, March 4, 1836. He was educated at the Commercial School, Montreal. He was formerly engaged in business as a wholesale grocer, but retired in 1897. He is a Director of the Dominion Cotton Mills. He married in 1861 Miss Susan Annie Walker, of Sorel. He was Mayor of the Village of St. Jean Baptiste for twenty years, and of Montreal in 1894-96. He was President of the Commissioners of Mount Royal Park; a Harbor Commissioner and Prefet of the County of Hochelaga for a period of ten years. He was first elected to the Legislative Assembly in 1886, but the election was declared void and a new election was held, April 28, 1888, when he was re-elected, and was also re-elected in 1890 and 1892, when he resigned. He was appointed to the Senate January 2, 1896. A Conservative.—*Montreal.*

HON. ALEXANDER VIDAL
(Sarnia.)

The Hon. Alexander Vidal was born in Bracknell, Berkshire, England, August 4, 1819. He is the son of the late Captain R. E. Vidal, R.N. The family originally came to England from Spain about the close of the 17th Century, and were Huguenot refugees, and removed from England to Canada in 1834. He was educated in the Royal Mathematical School, Christ's Hospital, London, England. He was married in December, 1847, to Catherine, eldest daughter of the late Capt. W. E. Wright, R.N., of Moore, Lambton. She died April 19, 1882. He practiced as a Provincial Land Surveyor in Ontario from 1843 until 1853 and was employed by the Government to survey and lay out the Township of Saugeen and the Town of Sault Ste. Marie, and to mark the boundaries of all the mining locations on the north shore of Lake Huron. He was Manager of the Sarnia Branch of the Bank of Upper Canada until 1867, and then of the Branch of the Bank of Montreal until 1875, when he retired from active business. He was County Treasurer of Lambton for 38 years, resigning in favor of his son in 1891. He is President of the Dominion Alliance for the suppression of the traffic in intoxicating liquors, having been annually re-elected to the position since 1876. He ran for the Commons at the general elections of 1872, but was defeated. He was elected and sat for St. Clair Division in the Legislative Council, Canada, from September, 1863, until the time of the Union. He was called to the Senate January 15, 1873. A Conservative.—*Sarnia, O.*

HON. ALEX. MACFARLANE, Q.C.
(Wallace.)

The Hon. Alex. Macfarlane was born at Wallace, N.S., June 17th, 1818, and is of Scottish descent, being a son of the late Hon. Donald Macfarlane. He was called to the Bar of Nova Scotia in Dec., 1844, and appointed Q.C. in June 1867. He married Anne, daughter of Mr. Amos Seaman, a resident of Minudie, N.S. He represented Cumberland in the Nova Scotia Assembly from 1856 until the time of the Union. He is President of the Spring Hill Mining Company, and is a Surrogate of Vice-Admiralty. Mr. Macfarlane was one of the delegates from Nova Scotia to the Colonial Conference in London to complete the terms of the Union in 1866 and 1867. He was a member of the Executive Council of N.S. from 1865 until the Union, and holds rank and precedence as such by patent from the Queen. He was appointed to the Senate October 10, 1870. A Conservative.—*Wallace, N.S.*

HON. FRANCIS CLEMOW.

(Rideau.)

The Hon. Francis Clemow was born at Three Rivers, Q., May 4, 1821. He is the son of Captain John Clemow, of H. M. 41st Regiment, who took part in the Battle of Queenston Heights. He was educated at the Upper Canada College, Toronto, and in 1840 he settled in Ottawa. He was married in 1847 to Margaret, daughter of the late Colonel Powell, of H.M. 101st Regiment. For several years he was engaged in the forwarding business, and then became an Official Assignee under the Insolvent Act. He is a Director of the Ottawa Electric Company, and since 1866 has held the position of Managing Director of the Ottawa Gas Company, and is still one of the Directors. He was a Member of the Ottawa City Council for two years, and for several years, from the initiation of the scheme until the completion of the Water works in 1875, was Chairman of the Board of Water Commissioners. For 25 years he has been chairman of the Ottawa Collegiate Institute. He was Grand Master of the Orangemen of Carleton County for eight years, and in 1892 he was Chairman of the Committee of the Whole in the Senate on the Bill to codify the Criminal Laws of Canada. He was called to the Senate, February 3, 1885. A Conservative.—*Ottawa.*

HOUSE OF COMMONS

HON. J. D. EDGAR.
(Speaker.)

The Hon. James David Edgar was born in the Eastern Townships, P.Q., August 10, 1841. He is a descendant of the elder branch of the Edgars of Keithoch, Forfarshire, Scotland. He was educated at Lennoxville and at the Belvidere School of Quebec. He married September, 1865, Matilda, second daughter of the late T. G. Ridout, Esq., of Toronto. He was called to the Bar, U. C., Michaelmas Term, 1864. In 1890, he was appointed a Q. C. by the Ontario Government. He has been a prolific writer in the newspapers and other periodicals, and is the author of The Insolvent Act of 1864, with Notes, Forms, etc. (Toronto, 1864). An Act to amend the Insolvent Act of 1864, with Annotations, Notes of Decisions, etc. (Toronto, 1865). The White Stone Canoe (Toronto, 1887). This Canada of Ours, and other Poems (1890). In 1874, he was sent by the Dominion Government to British Columbia to arrange for terms for the postponement of construction of the C.P.R. He was first elected to Parliament for the County of Monck at the general elections of 1872, and sat until the general elections of 1874. He was defeated in Centre Toronto in 1872. On August 22, 1884, he was elected by acclamation to his present seat, and was re-elected at general elections of 1887, 1891, 1896, and on August 19, 1896, he was unanimously elected Speaker of the House of Commons. A Liberal.—*Toronto.*

J. G. BOURINOT, C.M.G., LL.D., D.C.L., Litt. D., F.R.S.C.,
(Clerk of the House.)

John George Bourinot was born at Sydney, N.S., October 24, 1837, and is the eldest son of the late Hon. J. Bourinot, Senator, and grandson of Judge Marshall, son of a U. E. Loyalist, on his mother's side. He was educated under the tutorship of Rev. W. Y. Porter, and at Trinity College, Toronto, where he took the Wellington and other Scholarships. He studied law in Nova Scotia, and was subsequently connected with the newspaper press of Canada as Parliamentary Reporter and Editor. He established the Halifax *Reporter* in 1860, and was its chief editor for years. He was also Chief Official Reporter of the Nova Scotia Assembly from 1861 to Confederation. In 1868 he was appointed to Senate staff; Second Clerk Assistant House of Commons, April, 1873; First Clerk Assistant, February, 1879; Clerk of the House, December, 1880. Has received the following degrees: LL.D., Queen's University, Kingston, 1886; D.C.L., Trinity University, Toronto, 1888; D.C.L., King's College, Windsor, at Centennial Celebration in 1890; Docteur-es Lettres, Laval University, 1890, and D.C.L. at the Jubilee Celebration of Bishop's College, Lennoxville, 1895. Was nominated by Lord Lorne, Hon. Secretary of Royal Society in 1882, was President in 1892, and then re-elected Secretary continuously. Has lectured before Harvard, Johns Hopkins, Trinity and other Universities. Is a Member of the Council, and Examiner in Constitutional Law of Trinity; Member of the Council of American Historical Association and of the American Academy of Political Science; Hon. Member of the American Antiquarian Society; Hon. Fellow of Royal Colonial Institute, March, 1897. Dr. Bourinot is an authority on parliamentary practice, and author of a large work on Parliamentary Procedure, of "Federal Government in Canada," "How Canada is Governed," "The Story of Canada" (Nation's Series), "Cape Breton and its Memorials of the French Regime," "Procedure of Municipal Councils and Public Meetings," besides other works on constitutional and historical subjects. He is also a frequent contributor to "Johns Hopkins University Political Studies," the "Quarterly Review," "Blackwood," The Arena," and other English and American periodicals. Dr. Bourinot was created C.M.G. at New Year's, 1890.—*Ottawa.*

LIEUT.-COL. H. R. SMITH.
(Sergeant-at-Arms.)

Lieut.-Col. Smith was born December 30, 1843, at Kingston, Ont. He is the eldest son of the late Sir Henry Smith, Q.C., M.P., and Mary, daughter of the late Robert Talbot, Esq., of Kingston. Lieut-Col. Smith was educated at Kingston Grammar School, and is also a graduate of the Royal School of Artillery. He has been in the service of the Legislature since May 1, 1859, and in the Militia since May 2, 1863. Ensign and Lieutenant in Civil Service Rifle Regiment, 1866; Captain in 47th Batt., 1867; Major, 1875; A. D. C. to Gen. Sir E. Selby Smith, 1877, subsequently A. D. C. to Gen. Luard and the Marquess of Lansdowne; extra A. D. C. to the Earl of Derby; Honorary A. D. C. to the Earl of Aberdeen, 1894. Served as Major in Midland Regiment in Northwest Campaign. Mentioned in despatches and Medal. Appointed Deputy Sergeant at Arms, 1872; Sergeant at Arms, 1892. Is Lieut-Col. 14th P. W. O. Rifles. Married August 7, 1887, Mary Barrow, widow of the late Major Barrow.—*Ottawa*.

L. C. A. ANGERS.
(Charlevoix.)

Louis Charles Alphonse Angers was born at Malbaie, P.Q., being the son of Elie Angers, blacksmith, and Marie Perron. He was educated at Laval Normal School. He married in September, 1884, Dame Marie Julie Dumas, who is now dead. Mr. Angers is by profession an advocate. He was first elected to the House of Commons at the by-election of January, 1896, and re elected at the general elections of 1896, when he defeated the Conservative candidate, Mr. S. Cimon. A Liberal.—*Murray Bay, Q.*

J. G. H. BERGERON, B.C.L.
(Beauharnois.)

Joseph Gedeon Horace Bergeron was born at Rigaud on October 13, 1854. He is the son of the late Mr. T. R. Bergeron, notary, residing at Rigaud, County of Vaudreuil, Que., and of the late Leocadie Caroline Delphine Coursol, daughter of Gedeon Coursol, Esq., notary, of St. Andrews, Que. He was educated at the Jesuits' College, Montreal; he also followed a commercial course at the Montreal Business College, where he obtained a diploma. In March, 1877, he graduated a B. C. L. at McGill University. He was called to the Province of Quebec Bar in July, 1877. Mr. Bergeron was first elected to the Commons in January, 1879, through the death of the sitting member, Mr. M. Cayley, and at the general elections held in 1882 he was re-elected by acclamation, and was also re-elected at the general elections of 1887, 1891 and 1896. He married in July, 1890, Ada Josephine, daughter of the late Mr. R. Wall, of Montreal. In 1888 he was made Chairman of Committee on Standing Orders. In 1891 he was appointed Deputy Speaker and Chairman of Committees of the Commons, and continued so until April, 1896. He is a Member of the St. Denis Club, St. James' Club, St. Jerome Club and Le Club Canadien. A Liberal-Conservative.—*Montreal.*

THOMAS BAIN.

(South Wentworth.)

Thomas Bain was born on December 14, 1834, in the Parish of Denny, coming to Canada in 1837 with his father, the late Mr. Walter Bain, of Denny, Stirlingshire, Scotland, and settling in West Flamboro, Ont. He was educated in Canada. He married, June 25, 1874, Helen, second daughter of John Weir, Esq., of West Flamboro. Mr. Bain is a retired farmer. He was for several years Reeve of the Township of West Flamboro, and was also Warden of Wentworth in 1870. He was returned to Parliament at the general elections of 1872, and has sat there continuously since that year. A Reformer.—*Dundas, O.*

MAJOR THOMAS BEATTIE.

(London.)

Major Thomas Beattie is an Irishman, born in Belfast. Came to this country with his parents in 1848. Is a successful retired merchant. He is Senior Major of the 7th Fusiliers of London. Served through the North-West Rebellion with his Battalion. On three different occasions he has declined the command of the Regiment. He served as Alderman for London many years. Is Vice-President of London City Gas Company. Is a Director of the Agricultural Savings and Loan Company. On the retirement of Sir John Carling, K.C.M.G., he was unanimously selected by the Conservative party of London to become their candidate, and was elected in June, 1896, but his election was protested, 2,075 different charges being made against him and his friends, and after a trial, lasting 23 days (the longest on record) in the Election Court, in which the most eminent counsel of this County on both sides was engaged, the protest was dismissed with costs, and the Judges on the Bench declared not one charge against Major Beattie had been proven, and from the evidence produced it had been shown he had done all in his power to have a most fair and pure election. A Conservative.—*London, O.*

CHARLES BAZINET.

(Joliette.)

Charles Bazinet was born at Joliette on July 20, 1845. He was educated at Joliette College. He married Marie Philomene Courtois on October 21, 1867. Mr. Bazinet is a lumber merchant and is also proprietor of a saw mill. He was first elected to the House of Commons at the general elections of 1896, defeating Dr. V P. Lavallée, Conservative, by a vote of 1,769 to 1,453. A Liberal.—*St. Jean de Matha, Q.*

GEORGE H. BERTRAM.

(Centre Toronto.)

George Hope Bertram was born at Fenton Barns, Haddingtonshire, Scotland, March 12, 1847, and received his early education at the Parish School of Dirleton. He now devotes all his attention to the engine and shipbuilding business which he organized in 1892, now known as the Bertram Engine Works Co., Limited, of which he is at present President. Mr. Bertram has always taken an active part in municipal affairs, and especially in regard to municipal reforms; at the same time he has always shown a strong interest in Provincial and Dominion politics. He is a thorough business man, has a wide acquaintance with the business of the country generally, and a comprehensive grasp of all trade matters Mr. Bertram was for two years a member of the Council of the Toronto Board of Trade. He was returned to Parliament at a by-election in 1897 in the Liberal interest, but prefers the interests of the country to those of party, if ever the two should come into conflict. He favours a revenue tariff high enough to meet the requirements of the country as best suited to promote the general welfare of the people. He supports giving a preference on British imports, and is opposed to lowering the duties on American imports so long as Canadian products are practically excluded from the United States. A Liberal.—*Toronto, Ont.*

C. BEAUSOLEIL.

(Berthier.)

Cleophas Beausoleil was born at St. Felix de Valois, County of Joliette, June 19, 1845. He is of French descent, being a son of Joseph Beausoleil and Rose Ducharme. He was educated at Joliette College, Joliette. He was for some time on the staff of the Nouveau Monde, but in 1873 he founded and edited *Le Bien Public*. He afterwards became an Official Assignee in Insolvency. He was called to the Bar of the Province of Quebec in 1880. He is at present and has been for 10 years a member of the City Council of Montreal. He was first returned to Parliament at the general elections of 1887, and was re-elected at general election of 1891, and was elected by acclamation on June 16, 1896. A Liberal.—*Montreal.*

W. H. BENNETT.

(East Simcoe.)

William Humphrey Bennett was born on December 23, 1859, at Barrie, Ont., being of Irish descent on the side of his father, Humphrey Bennett, and of Scotch descent on the side of his mother, Anne A. Fraser. Educated at the Barrie Public and High Schools. Studied law, and called to the Bar of Ontario in 1881, since which date he has practiced, where he now resides, at Midland. Mr. Bennett was first elected Reeve of Midland in 1886, retaining the office for several years. Was a candidate for the representation of East Simcoe at the general elections, March of 1891, and defeated by P. H. Spohn. In 1892, after the unseating of Mr. Spohn, Mr. Bennett was elected by 32 majority. Again elected at the general elections of 1896 by a majority of 246, defeating H. H. Cook, Liberal, and Duncan Anderson, Patron, in a total of 6,501 votes. Moved the address in the House of Commons in 1895; unseated Dec. 23, 1896, and on Feb. 22, 1897, again defeated H. H. Cook, Liberal, by a majority of 127—votes polled, 6347. A Liberal-Conservative.—*Midland, O.*

ROBERT BEITH.

(West Durham.)

Robert Beith was born in the Township of Darlington, Ont. His father and mother were both natives of Campbelltown, Argyleshire, Scotland, where the family were engaged in the milling and farming business, and who subsequently came to Canada in 1835. He was educated in the public Schools of Darlington Township, and also in a private school at Bowmanville, and subsequently he took a course at a Commercial College in Toronto. He is unmarried. Mr Beith is by occupation a farmer and an importer of thoroughbred horses. He was first elected to the House of Commons at the general elections of 1891, and was re-elected at the general elections of 1896. A Liberal.—*Bowmanville, O.*

T. BLANCHARD.

(Gloucester.)

Theotime Blanchard was born at Caraquet, Gloucester County, N.B., May, 1846, and is of Acadian descent. He was educated at Caraquet. He married Marie Gauvin in March, 1867. He is by occupation a farmer and merchant; he taught school from 1861 until 1870, in which year he was appointed a J. P. From 1870 until 1876 he represented the County of Gloucester in the House of Assembly of New Brunswick, and again from 1892 until 1894 He was a Municipal Councillor for six years; he held the office of Inspector of Weights and Measures for Gloucester and Restigouche from 1876 until 1881, and also that of Preventive Officer in the Custom House at Caraquet from 1889 to 1892, when he resigned that office to offer for the Local House. He resigned his seat in the House of Assembly of N. B. in 1894, and was elected for the House of Commons for the first time to fill the vacancy caused by the appointment of the late K. F. Burns to the Senate; he was re-elected again by a large majority at the general elections held in 1896. A Conservative.—*Caraquet, N. B.*

N. A. BELCOURT.
(Ottawa City.)

Napoleon Antoine Belcourt was born in Toronto on September 15, 1860. He was educated at St. Joseph's Seminary, Three Rivers, and at Laval University, where he graduated with honors in Law in 1882. He married Hectorine, daughter of the Hon. Joseph Shehyn, of Quebec. He practiced law in Montreal for two years, and was in 1884 called to the Ontario Bar, and afterwards removed to Ottawa to practice. He is a member and also Secretary of the Faculty of Law of Ottawa University, and was made a Doctor of Laws of this University in 1895. He is also President of the Ottawa Liberal Reform Club, and is Vice-President of the Ontario Liberal Association. From June, 1894, to June, 1896, he held the offices of County Attorney and Clerk of the Peace for Carleton County, which he resigned to accept the candidature for the Capital. He was an unsuccessful candidate at the general elections held in 1891, and was first returned to Parliament at the general elections in 1896. A Liberal.—*Ottawa.*

M. E. BERNIER.
(St. Hyacinthe.)

Michel Esdras Bernier was born at St. Hyacinthe, September 27, 1841, and is the youngest son of the late Etienne Bernier of the same place. He was educated at the St. Hyacinthe Seminary. In June, 1867, he was admitted to practice as a notary, and is a member of the Notarial Board, Province of Quebec. He is now extensively engaged in farming, and for some years has been President of the St. Hyacinthe Agricultural Society. He married in November, 1865, Alida, daughter of the late Simeon Marchesseault, who in 1837 was a chief in the Rebellion, and was subsequently exiled to the Bermudas. He was first elected to the House of Commons in 1882, and was re-elected in 1887, 1891 and 1896. A Liberal.—*St. Hyacinthe, Que.*

ADAM C. BELL.
(Pictou.)

Adam Carr Bell was born at Pictou, N.S., November 11, 1847, his father being a native of Scotland and his mother of Nova Scotia. He was educated in the schools of New Glasgow, Sackville Academy and at the University of Glasgow. He married on September 4, 1873, Annie, daughter of Mr. John Henderson, of Albion Mines. Mr. Bell is by profession a druggist. He has been Warden of New Glasgow, and also a School Commissioner. He sat in the House of Assembly of Nova Scotia from 1878 until 1887, when he resigned his seat, and was defeated in running for Pictou in the House of Commons. He was a member of the Executive Council, and also Provincial Secretary in the Thompson Administration in Nova Scotia until that Government resigned in July, 1882, after which he was Leader of the Opposition until 1887. He was first elected to the House of Commons at the general elections of 1896. A Liberal-Conservative.—*New Glasgow, N.S.*

J. L. BETHUNE, M.D.
(Victoria, N.S.)

John Lemuel Bethune was born at Loch Lomond, County Richmond, N.S., in 1850, and is the eldest son of the late Roderick Bethune, formerly of Scotland, who emigrated to Cape Breton. He was educated at the Normal School, Truro, and at the University of Dalhousie, where he graduated an M.D., C.M. in 1875. He was Warden of Victoria for three years and was in 1881 Census Commissioner, and was a Member of the County Council for seven years. In January, 1885, he married Mary C., daughter of the late R. A. Jones, Esq. He is Lieut.-Col. of the 94th Batt. Argyle Highlanders, V. M., Commissioner of Schools, Coroner and a J. P. He sat in the N.S. House of Assembly from 1886 to June, 1896 when he resigned. He was first elected to the Commons at the general election of 1896. A Conservative.—*Baddeck, N.S.*

J. W. BELL.
(Addington.)

John William Bell was born in the Township of Camden, March 18, 1838. He is of Scottish descent, being the son of Daniel Fraser Bell, J.P. His grandfather was an officer in the British Army, and took part in the war of 1812, and his father also served as a volunteer in 1837. He was educated at the High School, Newburgh. He is by occupation a farmer. He was married December 5, 1869, to Julia, only daughter of Dr. Francis Purcell. He was Reeve of the Township of Camden for a period of seven years. He was Warden of the Counties of Lennox and Addington in 1879. He has been a Member of the Board of Audit for the said counties, and also Chairman of the Finance Committee. He was Grand Master of the Orange Provincial Grand Lodge of Ontario East for 1896, and holds the same office for the present year, and was elected 1st Vice-President of the Orange Triennial Council at the meeting held in Glasgow, July 14, 1897. He was first elected to Parliament at the general election of 1882. He was re-elected at the general election of 1887. He was defeated at the general election held in 1891, and was re-elected at the general election of 1896. A Conservative.—*Desmond, O.*

A. BRODER.
(Dundas.)

Andrew Broder was born in Franklin, County of Huntingdon, P. Q., in 1845. He is the son of William Broder of Kilfree, County of Sligo, Ireland; his mother was a native of Belfast, Ireland. He was educated in Huntingdon and at the Malone, N.Y., Academy. Mr. Broder was in business as a merchant until 1892, when he received the appointment of a Customs officer at Morrisburg. He held a seat in the Legislative Assembly of Ontario from 1875 until 1886. He was first elected to the House of Commons at the general election held in 1896. A Conservative.—*Morrisburg, O.*

B. M. BRITTON.
(Kingston.)

Byron Moffatt Britton was born at Gananoque, Leeds County, Ontario, September 3, 1833. His father came from New Hampshire and his mother from New York. Graduated in Arts at Victoria University. Is a barrister-at-law, and has been created a Queen's Counsel both by Ontario and Dominion patents. Has been a bencher of the Law Society since 1876. He held the office of County Crown Attorney for the County of Frontenac from 1883 to 1891, and that of Drainage Referee from 1891 to 1896. Mr. Britton has been Mayor of Kingston, Chairman of the Public School Board and one of the Governors of the Kingston General Hospital. He has been an exceedingly active and busy man in his profession and in many outside enterprises. He was a candidate for the representation of Cataraqui in 1864, but was defeated. He married, December 22, 1863, Mary E., eldest daughter of the late Hon. L. H. Holton. He was first elected to the House of Commons June 23, 1896, defeating his opponent, Mr. Donald C. McIntyre, by 1,671 votes to 1,519. A Liberal. —*Kingston O.*

L. P. BRODEUR.
(Rouville.)

Louis Philippe Brodeur was born at Beloeil, August 21, 1862. His ancestors emigrated from France to Canada about the 16th century, and he is the son of Toussaint Brodeur and Justine Lambert. He was educated at the College of St. Hyacinthe. In June, 1887, he married Emma, daughter of Mr. J. R. Brillon, notary of Beloeil. He received the degree of LL.B. at Laval University, and was admitted to the Province of Quebec Bar in July, 1884. He was first elected to the House of Commons at the general elections held in 1891, and was re-elected at the general elections of 1886. In August, 1896, he was elected Deputy Speaker and Chairman of the Committee. A Liberal.—*Montreal.*

J. H. N. BOURASSA.
(Labelle.)

J. H. N. Bourassa was born in Montreal, September 1, 1868. He is the son of Napoleon Bourassa, who was for several years director of *La Revue Canadienne* of Montreal, and was also author of various works on Art, and of the book, "Jacques et Marie," an Episode of the deportation of the Acadians in 1755; and of Azelie, daughter of Louis Joseph Papineau, the famous French Canadian agitator. He was educated in Montreal by private tuition. He removed to Montebello in 1886, where his great-grandfather established, in 1798, the first settlement in what is now known as Ottawa County. He was Mayor of Montebello from 1890 to 1894, and was editor and proprietor of *L'Interprete* from 1893 and subsequently of *Le Ralliement*. He was President of the Agricultural Society of the Eastern part of Ottawa County for two years. He was first elected to the Commons in 1896. A Liberal.—*Montebello, Q.*

A. BOURBONNAIS, M.D.
(Soulanges.)

Augustin Bourbonnais, M. D., was born at St. Clet, Soulanges Co., March 19, 1850. He is a descendant of a family emigrated from France with Lasalle in 1644, which landed at Lachine, part of which proceeded to the counties of Vaudreuil and Soulanges, taking up farming, and the other part to Bourbonnais, Ill., U. S. A. He was educated at the Seminary of Ste. Thérèse, and graduated a B. A. in June, 1872. He also graduated an M.D. at Laval University, Quebec, in 1875. He practised his profession for two years in Syracuse, N.Y., and then removed to Coteau Landing, where he still resides. He was an unsuccessful candidate at a by-election held in December, 1892. He was first elected to the House of Commons at the general election held in 1896, when he defeated Mr. E. Lanthier, the Conservative candidate, by a vote of 1054 to 861. A Liberal.—*Coteau Landing, Q.*

R. L. BORDEN.
(Halifax.)

Robert Laird Borden was born June 26, 1854, at Grand Pré, in Kings County, N. S., and is a son of Andrew Borden, of Grand Pré, whose grandfather emigrated to Nova Scotia from the United States about 1870. He was educated at Acadia Villa School in Kings County. Was admitted to the Bar in Nova Scotia in 1878. Mr. Borden is now the senior partner in the firm of Borden, Ritchie, Parker & Chisholm. He was appointed a Q. C. in 1890; is President of the Nova Scotia Barristers' Society, and has several times been Vice-President of the same Society. In politics he was a Liberal (although not taking an active part) until the year 1886, when he left that party on the question of the attempted secession of the Province of Nova Scotia from the Confederation. From that time until 1896 he supported the Conservative party, but took no very active part until 1896, when he accepted the nomination as a candidate for the City and County of Halifax, and was elected at the head of the poll. A Liberal-Conservative.—*Halifax, N.S.*

A. A. BRUNEAU.
(Sorel.)

Arthur Aimé Bruneau was born at St. Athanase, Province of Quebec, on March 4, 1864. He was educated at the College of the Sacred Heart, Sorel, and the Jesuit College in Montreal. On October 11, 1887, he married at Quebec, Arzelie, daughter of J. B. Cloutier, professor of Laval University. He is by profession an advocate. From 1885 until 1887 he was Secretary of Le Club National of Montreal. He is now the Vice-President of the St. Jean Baptiste Society of Sorel, and is also the President of Le Club des Jeunes Liberaux de Richelieu. He was first elected to the House of Commons for Richelieu at a by-election January 11, 1892, and was re-elected at the last general elections, defeating the Hon. A. Desjardins, Minister of Public Works, by 134 majority. A Liberal.—*Sorel, Q.*

J. P. BROWN.
(Chateauguay.)

James Pollock Brown was born at Beau River, April 4, 1841. He is the son of David Brown and Jean Pollock, both of Renfrewshire, Scotland. He was educated at the Elementary Schools and also at United States Business College at New Haven, Conn. On February 19, 1869, he married Miss Margaret Stewart. Mr. Brown is a general store keeper, farmer and grist-miller. He was first elected to Parliament at the general election of 1891, and was re-elected at the last general election, defeating C. Lecavalier, Conservative, by a vote of 1594 to 894. A Liberal.—*St. Chrysostome, Q.*

LEONARD BURNETT.
(South Ontario.)

Leonard Burnett is a native of Yorkshire, England, and was born April 5, 1845, the families of both his father, Thomas Burnett, and his mother, Hannah Dickenson, having been farmers. He was educated at Greenwood Public School and Whitby High School. For three years he was a teacher, and since that time has been a farmer. He has held the offices of County Councillor, Deputy Reeve and Reeve of the Township of Reach, and has been a school trustee for twenty-five successive years and secty.-treas. during that term; also auditor for the County of Ontario for 3 years. Appointed a J. P. in 1885. He married January 5, 1870, Sarah Jane, daughter of the late James Dryden and sister of the Hon. John Dryden, who died on March 11, 1896. Mr. Burnett has had to work his own way in the world. He is an extensive farmer and large breeder of Durham cattle, Shropshire sheep, Clydesdale horses and Berkshire hogs, and believes in the best stock as being the most profitable. He was first elected to Parliament June 23, 1896 A Liberal.—*Greenbank, O.*

HEWITT BOSTOCK.

(Yale and Cariboo.)

Hewitt Bostock was born at the Hermitage, Walton Heath, Epsom, England. He is the son of Samuel Bostock, who was a member of the London Stock Exchange. He was educated by private tuition at Brighton and Guilford, and in 1882 he entered Trinity College, Cambridge, where he graduated in 1885 with mathematical honors. He was called to the Bar at Lincoln's Inn in 1888. He was married June 12, 1890, to Lizzie Jean McCombie, third daughter of Hugh Cowie, Esq., Q.C., of Ithandale, Wimbledon, Surrey, and Chancellor of the Diocese of Durham. He settled in British Columbia in October, 1893, where he is engaged in ranching, and is also proprietor of *The Province*, a weekly journal. He was first elected to the House of Commons at the general election held in 1896. A Liberal.—*Victoria, B.C.*

WILLIAM S. CALVERT.

(West Middlesex.)

William Samuel Calvert was born March 3, 1857, in the Township of Warwick, County of Lambton, Ont. His father came from the North of Ireland, and his mother from Glasgow, Scotland, settling first in the County of Lanark, but afterwards moving to Lambton. He was educated at the Public Schools there and also at the Waterford Seminary. He is a merchant by occupation, and among the public offices held is that of Reeve of the Township of Metcalfe from 1886 to 1894, and Warden of the County of Middlesex in 1894. He is also a prominent Free Mason, and was District Deputy Grand Master for the St. Claire district in 1889. Mr. Calvert was married December 17, 1879, to Cora, daughter of Mr. James G. Sutherland, merchant of Napier. He has always taken a keen interest in politics, and was first returned to Parliament at the general elections of 1896. A Liberal—*Napier, O.*

M. C. CAMERON, Q.C.

(West Huron.)

Malcolm Colin Cameron was born in Perth, Ont., April 12, 1832. He was educated at the Knox College, Toronto. He has held several public offices, such as Town Councillor, Reeve and Mayor of Goderich. In 1860 he was called to the Bar of Upper Canada, and in March, 1876, was appointed a Q.C. by the Ontario Government. He married, in May, 1855, Jessie H., daughter of Dr. John McLean, who was formerly in the Royal Navy. He held a seat in the Commons for South Huron from 1867 until 1882, when he ran for West Huron and was elected. In 1887 he was defeated, and was re-elected in 1891, but was unseated in 1892, and was defeated at the by-election held that year. He was re-elected at a by-election in 1896, and also at the general elections in 1896. A Liberal.—*Goderich, O.*

ARCHIBALD CAMPBELL.

(Kent, Ont.)

Archibald Campbell was born in the Township of Howard, County of Kent, April 27, 1845. He is the son of the late Neil Campbell, who emigrated to New-York State from Argyleshire, Scotland, about 1812, and who removed to the Township of Howard in 1830. He was educated at the Common and High Schools. He is engaged in business as a merchant miller. In February, 1871, he married Miss Burk, of Colona, California. He has for several years been a member of the Town Council of Chatham, Deputy Reeve of Chatham, and Chairman of the Finance Commitee. He was first elected to the House of Commons at the general elections of 1887, but was unseated in November, 1887. He was re-elected in May, 1888, 1891 and 1896. A Liberal.—*Toronto Junction, O.*

HENRY CARGILL.

(East Bruce.)

Henry Cargill was born in the Township of Nassagaweya, County of Halton. His father and mother were both natives of the county of Antrim, Ireland, and emigrated to Canada and settled in the County of Halton. He was educated there and at Queen's College, Kingston, Ont. Mr. Cargill is extensively engaged as a merchant and in the manufacture of lumber. He married in March, 1864, Margaret Davidson, of the County of Halton. He was Reeve of the Township of Greenock, and has been Postmaster of Cargill. He was first elected to the House of Commons in February, 1887, but resigned and was re-elected in April, 1887. In 1891 he was defeated, but was re-elected at a by election in 1892 and at the general elections of 1896. A Conservative.—*Cargill, O.*

ALEXANDER W. CARSCALLEN.

(North Hastings.)

Alexander Williamson Carscallen was born in the Township of North Fredericksburg, County of Lennox, Ontario, October 14, 1844. His father, Edward Riggs Carscallen, was a lieutenant in the Canadian Militia, and was on active service during the Rebellion of 1837. Mr. Carscallen also comes of military stock through his grandfather, who held a Captain's commission in the British Army, and during the Revolutionary War abandoned his property at Albany, N.Y., and came to Canada.

The subject of our sketch was educated at Napanee Academy and the University of Nashville, Tenn., U.S. His business is that of a private banker. He has been a Councillor and Reeve of his Township and Chairman of the School Board. Is also a Justice of the Peace. He was first returned to Parliament at a by-election held December 30, 1892, on the appointment of Sir Mackenzie Bowell to the Senate, and was again returned at the general elections of 1896. Mr. Carscallen was married November 16, 1874, to Marcia Pringle. A Conservative.—*Marmora, O.*

HON. SIR ADOLPHE CARON, K.C.M.G., Q.C., P.C.

(Three Rivers.)

The Hon. Sir Joseph Philippe René Adolphe Caron was born in Quebec City, December 24, 1843, and is the eldest surviving son of the late Hon. R. E. Caron. He was educated at the Quebec Seminary, Laval University and the University of McGill, where he graduated B.C.L. in 1865. He was called to the Bar of Lower Canada in 1865, and was appointed Q. C. in May, 1879. He married in June, 1867, Alice, only daughter of the late Hon. Francois Baby. In November, 1880, he was sworn of the Privy Council and appointed Minister of Militia, holding that portfolio until January 25, 1892, when he was appointed Postmaster-General. He was a member of the Abbott, Thompson and Bowell Ministries, but retired in April, 1896. He was first elected to Parliament for Quebec County in 1873, and was re-elected in 1874, 1878, and upon his appointment to office, and was re-elected in 1882 and 1887. He was created a K.C.M.G. in August, 1885. In 1891 he was elected for Rimouski, and at the last general election for his present seat. A Liberal-Conservative.—*Ottawa.*

HENRY G. CARROLL.

(Kamouraska.).

Henry George Carroll was born in Kamouraska, January 31, 1865, and is the son of Michael Burke Carroll and Marguerite Campbell. He was educated at Ste. Anne de Lapocatiere College and at Laval University, Quebec, where he graduated an LL.B., in July, 1889. He was admitted to the Bar of the Province of Quebec, July 3, 1889, and subsequently practiced his profession at Fraserville, Que. He was married June 1, 1891, to Amazelie, daughter of L. Boulanger, a merchant of Ste. Agathe de Lotbinière. He was first elected to the House of Commons for Kamouraska, in 1891, and was re-elected at the last general elections. A Liberal.—*Fraserville, Q.*

G. E. CASEY, B.A., J.P.
(West Elgin.)

George Elliot Casey was born in the Township of Southwold, County of Elgin, March 24, 1850. He is the son of the late William Casey, from Mullingar, County Westmeath, Ireland, and his mother, Sarah Elliot, came from Omagh, County of Tyrone, Ireland. He was educated at the St. Thomas High School, and at the University of Toronto, where he received the degree of B.A. in 1871. He is a gentleman farmer. He was married in 1877 to Sarah Isabella, daughter of the late J. L. Biggar, who represented East Northumberland. He is interested in mining developments. He has represented West Elgin, Ontario, continuously since the general election of 1872. He is the youngest member ever elected. He was the Government Whip under the Mackenzie Administration, and was also Liberal Whip for several years after, when he resigned in favor of the late James Trow. Since 1875 he has consistently advocated for reform of the Civil Service similar to the English System. He succeeded in getting his plan endorsed by the several committees, and by the Civil Service Commission of 1880. He was elected at the general elections of 1874, 1878, 1882, 1887, 1891 and 1896. A Reformer.—*Fingal, O.*

L. A. CHAUVIN.
(Terrebonne.)

Leon Adolphe Chauvin was born at Terrebonne July 20, 1861. He was educated at the Montreal College. He is by profession an advocate, and is now a member of the law firm of Archambault & Chauvin, Montreal. He was married in 1889 to Miss Berthe Gagnon, of Quebec. In 1891 he held the office of Chief Census Officer for the Province of Quebec, District of Montreal, and he was Secretary of " La Société Canadienne d'Economie Sociale." He was first elected to the House of Commons at the general election held in 1896, when he defeated the Liberal candidate, Mr. P. F. E. Petit, by a majority of 128 votes. A Liberal-Conservative.—*Montreal.*

P. A. CHOQUETTE, LL.B.

(Montmagny.)

Philippe Auguste Choquette was born at Belœil, County of Verchères, January 6, 1854. He is the son of Mr. Joseph Choquette and Mrs. Marie T. Audet. He was educated at the St. Hyacinthe College, and at Laval University, graduating a B.C.L. in 1880, after having previously won the Silver Medal donated by Lord Lorne. In August, 1883, he married Marie, daughter of Mr. A. Bender, Prothonotary, and a grand-daughter of the late Sir E. P. Taché. Mr. Choquette is engaged in practice as an advocate, but has been for some years contributing to the Press, and is the publisher of a newspaper. At the general elections of 1882 he was a candidate for his present seat, but was unsuccessful. He was first elected to the Commons at the general elections of 1887, and was re-elected at those of 1891 and 1896. A Liberal.—*Montmagny, Q.*

E. COCHRANE, J.P.

(East Northumberland.)

Edward Cochrane was born in the Township of Cramahe, Ont, January 1, 1834. He is the son of James Cochrane, of Yorkshire, England, and Mary Davis, of Wexford, Ireland, both of whom emigrated to the Township of Cramahe, Ont., in 1826. He was educated at Colborne, Ont. In August, 1856, he married, first, Miss M. Hicks, and second, in April, 1875, Ellen Louisa, daughter of Stephen Thom, Esq. He has held the position of Reeve, Deputy Reeve and Councillor of the Township of Cramahe for many years, and was, in 1880, Warden of the United Counties of Northumberland and Durham. He was first elected to the Commons at the general elections of 1882, and was defeated in 1887. The sitting member being unseated, a new election was held in December, 1887, when Mr. Cochrane was elected, but the election being declared void another was held in November, 1888, and he was re-elected. He was also re-elected in 1891 and 1896. A Conservative.—*Edville, O.*

THOMAS CHRISTIE, M.D.
(Argenteuil.)

Dr. Thomas Christie was born in the City of Glasgow, Scotland, March 8, 1824, and was the third son of John Christie and Elizabeth Nicol, both of Stirlingshire, Scotland. He came to Canada in 1827, and studied medicine at McGill College, where he graduated M. D. in 1848. In 1847 he acted as Assistant Surgeon at Point St. Charles during the ship fever scourge in that year, and ever since then has been actively engaged in the practice of his profession, in which he has earned a deservedly high reputation. Dr. Christie was for some time Warden of Argenteuil, and for several years Chairman of the Board of School Commissioners for the Parish of St. Jerusalem D'Argenteuil. He was first returned to Parliament for his present seat by acclamation on December 31, 1875; was re-elected in 1878, but unseated for the act of an agent. He was again re-elected in 1891, and again at the last general elections. A Liberal.—*Lachute, Q.*

E. F. CLARKE.
(Toronto West.)

E. F. Clarke was elected one of the Conservative members for West Toronto at the last election. He is a native of Bailieboro, County Caven, Ireland, where he was born April 24, 1850. His father was Richard Clarke and his mother Eleanor Reynolds. He received his education at the National Model School, Bailieboro. He came early in life to Canada and established a flourishing printing and publishing business in Toronto, where he issued *The Sentinel*. He is at present the President and Managing Director of the Excelsior Life Insurance Company. Mr. Clarke is highly esteemed in the Queen City, as is evidenced by the fact that he has been four consecutive times elected to the Mayoralty. He has also been a member of the Ontario Legislature for two terms. Mr. Clarke is a man of strong convictions and fearless in stating and defending them. —*Toronto, O.*

J. CLANCY.
(Bothwell.)

James Clancy was born in the Township of Mosa, County of Middlesex, Ont, July 21, 1844, being the second son of the late Patrick Clancy, a native of the County of Roscommon, Ireland. He was married on July 28, 1868, to Emily, daughter of the late Alex. McIntosh. Mr. Clancy is by occupation a farmer. He has been a member of the Town Council of Dresden and has also been Reeve of Chatham on several occasions. He sat in the Legislative Assembly of Ontario from 1883 until 1894, in which year he was an unsuccessful candidate. He was first elected to the House of Commons at the general election held in 1896, when he defeated the Hon. D. Mills, Liberal, by a vote of 2,587 to 2,528. A Conservative.—*Wallaceburg, O.*

ALBERT J S. COPP.
(Digby.)

Albert James Smith Copp was born at Amherst, N.S. He is of English descent. His father was Thomas Copp, a Loyalist, who came from the United States. He was educated in Amherst Academy and also at Dorchester and Sackville, N.B. He married in 1881, Eliza, youngest daughter of James A. Dennison, Esq., of Digby. He was called to the Nova Scotia Bar in 1879. He has been the Crown Prosecutor for the County of Digby since 1887, and has achieved an enviable reputation, and ranks

among the foremost of the Criminal lawyers of Nova Scotia. He has been engaged in many notable criminal trials. The last notable case was the prosecution of Peter Wheeler for the murder of Annie Kempton, at Bear River, Digby County, on the 29th of January, 1896, when upon purely circumstantial evidence he was found guilty. Mr. Copp is a namesake of Sir Albert James Smith, Minister of Marine and Fisheries during Alexander MacKenzie's administration. He was first returned to Parliament at the general elections of 1896, having defeated his opponent by a majority of 45. A Liberal.—*Digby, N.S.*

THOMAS C. CASGRAIN.
(Montmorency.)

Thomas Chase Casgrain was born in Detroit, Mich., U.S.A., July 28, 1852, and is the son of Senator C. E Casgrain, M.D., and of Charlotte M. Chase, of Windsor, Ont. He was educated at the Seminary of Quebec and Laval University, where he graduated as Master of Laws in 1887, and took the Dufferin Medal. He was married May 15, 1878, to Marie Louise, daughter of Alex. LeMoine, Esq., and is by profession an advocate and was appointed Q.C. in 1887. He is Professor of Criminal Law of Laval University. He was Junior Counsel for the Crown at the trial of Louis Riel and other rebels at Regina, in July, 1885. He held a seat in the Quebec Legislature from 1886 to 1896, in which year he resigned, and was elected to the House of Commons. He was appointed to the Executive Council of the Province of Quebec in December, 1891, and was Attorney-General in the DeBoucherville Government, and was reappointed to the same office in the Taillon Administration. Was Chairman of the Commission which revised the Code of Civil Procedure of the Province of Quebec (1893-1897). Is the author of the Quebec Election Act of 1895, and of several other important laws. A Conservative.—*Montreal.*

JOHN FERGUSON.
(South Renfrew.)

John Ferguson was born at Granart, Argyleshire, April 17, 1840, and is the second son of the late Archibald Ferguson and Margaret Barr, both of whom were natives of Argyleshire, Scotland. In 1847 he came to Canada and settled in Admaston. Mr. Ferguson is now extensively engaged in lumbering and farming. He was first elected to the House of Commons at a by-election held in August, 1887. He was re elected at the general elections held in 1891 and at the general elections of 1896. An Independent-Conservative.—*Admaston, O.*

JOHN CHARLTON.
(North Norfolk.)

John Charlton was born at Wheatland, near Caledonia, N.Y., February 3, 1829. His father was an Englishman, who came from Newcastle-upon Tyne in 1824, and his mother was of Scotch descent. He was educated at the McLaren Grammar School, Caledonia, N.Y., and at Springville Academy, Springville, N.Y. He came to Canada with his father's family in 1849. He is a lumberman and farmer, doing an extensive business in the lumber trade in Canada, Michigan and New York. He was first returned to Parliament in 1872, and has retained his seat there ever since, having completed twenty-five years of continuous service August 5, 1897. He was Chairman of the Royal Mining Commission of Ontario in 1889. Mr. Charlton was the promoter of what is known as the "Charlton Act," a measure designed to afford protection to women and girls, which fixed the age of consent at sixteen years, making the seduction of a female under that age a misdemeanor, and providing for the punishment of seduction under promise of marriage. He has for many years sought to secure legislation against Sunday newspapers, and to recognize Sunday rest as a civil right. He is also interested in fiscal legislation, and is deeply impressed with the importance of Church and Sabbath School work. He is regarded as the friend of moral legislation. A Liberal.—*Lynedoch, O.*

J. F. GUITE.
(Bonaventure.)

Jean Francois Guité was born at Maria, P.Q., March 30, 1852. Is the son of Francois Guité, farmer, and Rachel Ahier; a nephew of the late Vital Tetu, M.P.P., and full cousin to Hon. C. A. P. Pelletier, Speaker of the Senate of Canada. He was educated at the Laval Normal School, Quebec, where he succeeded in gaining a diploma, and is by occupation a general merchant. He was married to Miss Madeleine Caron, of Percé, Gaspé. He was elected to Parliament for his present seat, March 17, 1897.—*Maria, Q*

MAHLON K. COWAN.

(South Essex.)

Mahlon K. Cowan was born May 10, 1863, in Mersea Township, Essex County, Ontario. Descended from Irish and English parentage, his father coming from the North of Ireland to Canada in 1842. He was educated at the Brantford and Collingwood Collegiate Institutes, and entered upon the study of law under the Honorable A. S. Hardy, Premier of Ontario, in 1885; graduated in 1890, and commenced the practice of his profession in Windsor. Is now a partner of the law firm of Clarke, Cowan, Bartlet & Bartlet, of that city. Was nominated before the general elections of 1896, and was successful in the contest that followed over his opponent, Dr. King, Conservative, by a majority of 183, which is a record majority for the Constituency in Dominion politics, it never having been carried by a majority of over sixty either way since the County was divided into North and South Ridings. A Liberal.—*Windsor, O.*

FRANCIS T. FROST.

(Leeds and Grenville.)

Father and mother of Vermont parentage, resided in N. Y. State, up to 1834, when they moved into Canada, and subsequently settled at Smith's Falls, Ont. Born at Smith's Falls, December 21, 1843. Educated at the Grammar School there, and at St. Lawrence Academy, Potsdam, N.Y. Married June 3, 1868, Maria E., daughter of the late C. Powell, Esq., of Madrid, N.Y. Is a manufacturer of agricultural implements. Was Reeve of Smith's Falls from January 1, 1876, until its erection into a town, January 1, 1883, when he became its first Mayor. Was Warden of the County of Lanark in 1878 and 1879, and has been a School Trustee for four years. Was an unsuccessful candidate for the House of Commons at general election 1878, 1881 and 1891, and for Legislative Assembly, Ont., 1886. First returned to Parliament at general election 1896. A Liberal.—*Smith's Falls, O.*

L. N. CHAMPAGNE.

(Wright.)

L. N. Champagne was born in St. Eustache, County of Two Mountains, on November 21, 1860. He is a son of Honorable Charles L. Champagne, Judge of the Circuit Court in Montreal. He completed his education in St. Hyacinthe College, and followed a legal course in Laval University of Montreal, where he obtained the degrees of that institution. He studied law under Messrs. Girouard & Wurtele, and was admitted to the Bar in July, 1882. He settled in Hull, and for two years practiced alone. In 1884 he formed a partnership with Mr. Alfred Rochon, Q.C. and ex-M.P.P., also of Hull, and the firm enjoys a large clientèle. Married September 7, 1885, Aldée Chevrier, daughter of Alexandre Chevrier, Esq., of Hull. Mr. Champagne was elected an Alderman of that City in 1889, and Mayor in 1892. In 1896 he was again elected Mayor. He is the Bâtonnier of the Bar of the District of Ottawa. On the resignation of Mr. Devlin, the member for the County of Wright, to accept the position of Emigration Commissioner for Ireland, Mr. Champagne was elected for that constituency. A Liberal.—*Hull, Q.*

THOMAS EARLE.

(Victoria City, B. C.)

Thomas Earle was born in Leeds, Ont., September 27, 1837, and received his education in the Common Schools. His parents came from Ireland about 1820, and settled in Leeds. Removing to British Columbia, Mr. Earle started business there as a general merchant, and in 1875 married Miss Elizabeth Mason. Mr. Earle has been a member of the municipal Council of Victoria, and in that capacity has rendered important service to the city; he was also a member of the Council of the Board of Trade. At a by-election held in October, 1889, he was first returned to Parliament by acclamation, and at the general election of 1891 and 1896 was again re-elected. A Conservative.—*Victoria, B.C.*

HENRY CORBY.

(West Hastings.)

Henry Corby was born in Belleville, May 2, 1851, and is of English descent, his parents having come to Canada from Hanwell, County of Middlesex, England. He was educated at the Common School in Belleville, and at the Rockwood Academy, Ontario, and he also took a commercial course at Bryant & Stratton's Commercial College, Toronto. He married on Sept. 23, 1872, Maria Courtney, of Belleville. He is in business as a distiller and importer of fine wines and liquors. He was foreman of No. 1 Hose Company, and was also First Assistant Chief of Belleville Fire Department. He is President of the Rambler's Bicycle Club, of the Bay of Quinté Yacht Club, and also of the Forest and Stream and Cricket Club. He was a Director of the Bay of Quinté Agricultural Exhibition. He was Vice-President of the Bay of Quinté Bridge Company and is also President of Belleville Hotel Company. He was first elected to Parliament at a by-election held March 17, 1888, by acclamation, and also elected again in 1891 and 1896. A Conservative.—*Belleville, O.*

J. L. E. DUGAS.

(Montcalm.)

Joseph Louis Euclide Dugas was born in Montcalm, August 30, 1861, and is the son of the late Firman Dugas, who represented Montcalm in the House of Commons for several years, and who was also a member of the Legislative Assembly of Quebec for six years. He was educated at the Joliette and Ottawa Colleges. He married, January 30, 1883, Lizzie, daughter of the late Thomas Rowan, J. P. Mr. Dugas is by occupation a farmer, and has been a School Commissioner since 1889. He was first elected to Parliament at the general elections of 1891, but, his election being declared void, he was re-elected at a by-election held March 3, 1892. He was again re-elected at the general elections held in 1896. A Conservative.—*Montcalm, Q.*

HON. JOHN COSTIGAN, J.P., P.C.

(Victoria, N.B.)

Born at St. Nicholas, P. Q., February 1, 1835. Educated at St. Ann's College. Married to a daughter of Mr. John H. Ryan, of Grand Falls, N.B., in 1855. Was a Judge of the Inferior Court Common Pleas for Victoria County and Registrar of Deeds and Wills for the same County. First selected for present seat in 1861 for the Legislature of N.B. In the election of 1866, though having received a majority of the votes polled authorized the Returning Officer to declare his opponent elected to avoid a serious riot. Elected to the House of Commons in 1867 and at every general election since. Was appointed Minister of Inland Revenue in Sir John Macdonald's Cabinet, May, 23, 1882. Held that portfolio under Sir John Abbott's Government. Held the position of Secretary of State under Sir John Thompson and that of Minister of Marine and Fisheries in Sir Mackenzie Bowell's Administration until the resignation of the Government, July 8, 1896. Took a prominent part in the New Brunswick School Question. In 1882 moved an address to Her Majesty in favour of Home Rule for Ireland. It was carried unanimously in the Commons and in the Senate, and only six votes dissenting. A Conservative and strong advocate of the faithful observance of the rights of minorities guaranteed by the Constitution.—*Grand Falls, N.B.*

JOSEPH GAUTHIER.

(L'Assomption.)

Joseph Gauthier was born at St. Lin, Province of Quebec, in 1842, and received his education and training there. He combines the business of merchant with that of farmer, in both of which occupations he has been very successful. He first engaged in politics in 1887, at the general election of which year he was elected to Parliament, but was unseated. He was again re-elected in April, 1888. At the general election of 1891 he was re-elected, but was unseated for the second time. At the last general election, in 1896, he was again re-elected.—*Laurentides, Q.*

T. D. CRAIG.
(Durham East.)

Thomas Dixon Craig was born in London, England, but was brought to Canada while still an infant. He was educated at Toronto University, from which he graduated in 1864, with the distinction of Gold Medalist in Metaphysics. Mr. Craig sat in the Legislative Assembly of Ontario from 1886 to 1890. While a member of that body he introduced the motion respecting French Schools in the province, which was the cause of Hon. Oliver Mowat appointing a Commission on the subject. At the general elections of 1890 for the Ontario Legislature, the question brought forward in the motion formed one of the principal planks of the Conservative Party. He was first elected to the Dominion Parliament in 1891. He is in favor of Prohibition, and also strongly opposed Remedial Legislation with respect to Manitoba Separate Schools, and at the general elections in 1896 was again re-elected. A Liberal-Conservative.—*Port Hope, O.*

G. W. GANONG.
(Charlotte.)

Gilbert White Ganong was born at Springfield, King's County, N. B., and is a descendant of Jean Guenon, a Huguenot of France, who on April 2, 1657, sailed from Amsterdam, landing at Flushing, Long Island, and is also a descendant of Thomas Ganong, a U. E. Loyalist, who arrived at St. John, N.B., in 1783. He was educated at Springfield. Mr. Ganong is President of Ganong Bros. Ltd., the largest confectionery manufacturing establishment in Eastern Canada. He married in October, 1876, Maria F., daughter of Mr. J. B. Robinson. He is a member of the Senate of the University of New Brunswick, and has been a member of the Board of School Trustees of St. Stephen for ten years. He was first elected to the House in 1896. An Independent-Conservative.—*St. Stephen, N.B.*

N. F. DAVIN.

(West Assiniboia.)

Nicholas Flood Davin was born at Kilfinane, County of Limerick. Ireland, June 13, 1843, being descended from families long settled in Tipperary. Married July 25, 1895, Elizabeth, daughter of James Reid, Ottawa. He was educated at Queen's University, Ireland, and at College affiliated to the University of London. He is by profession a Barrister. He was called to the Bar of the Middle Temple, London, in 1868, and was subsequently called to the Bar of Ontario, and is also a Barrister of the North-West Territories. He was appointed a Q.C. by the Dominion Government on October 27, 1892. Mr. Davin has also had considerable experience as a journalist, having been War Correspondent for the Dublin *Irish Times* and the London *Standard* during the Franco-German War, being wounded at the siege of Montmedy. In March, 1883, he established the Regina *Leader*. He is the author of several well-known works in prose and verse. He ran for Haldimand in 1878, but was defeated. In 1879 went to Washington as Commissioner to enquire into the system in the United States of educating Indian children; thence he visited the Agencies; thence went to Winnipeg and conferred with Archbishop Taché, Père Lacombe, the Hon. James Mackay, Messrs. Geo. and John McTavish and others, and visited reserves, and it is on his report the present system of educating Indian children in the North West is based. He in Parliament has been the means of removing a number of North-West grievances, and obtaining concessions culminating in the Act of 1897, giving them responsible government. On March 11, 1897, at a grand convention at Regina, he was elected President of the Liberal-Conservative Association for the whole Territories. He was first returned in 1887, and re-elected in 1891 and 1896. A Conservative.—*Regina, N.W.T.*

A. M. DECHENE.

(L'Islet.)

Arthur Miville Dechene was born in 1848, his father being Miville Dechene, and his mother Luce Talbot, both of the same County. His father ran twice for the County of L'Islet, but without success. His brother, Gilbert Miville, has represented the County in the Legislative Assembly of Quebec for the last ten years, being 25 years of age at the time of his first election, and is presently the Honorable Minister of Agriculture. Mr. Dechene was educated in St. Anne's College, and married in 1871 Miss Aurore Ouellet, of Ste. Louise. He resided for some time at Seven Islands, Me., on one of his farms, but now lives at the seigniorial manor of St. Roch des Aulnaies. He also owns the seigniory of St. Roch, Ste. Anne and St. Francois, Island of Orleans, County of Montmorency. He is a lumber merchant, and carries on business in the State of Maine and the Province of New Brunswick. Was first returned to Parliament at the general elections of 1896.—*Village des Aulnaies, Q.*

THOMAS FORTIN.

(Laval.)

Thomas Fortin was born at St. Francis, County of Beauce, and is descended from an old French family which resided near Rouen, France. He was educated in the Elementary School of the locality, and was afterwards under private tuition in Quebec and Montreal. He studied for the law, and after passing through a brilliant course was admitted to the Bar of the Province of Quebec in 1882. In 1888 he was appointed Professor of Civil and Municipal Law in McGill University, which important position he still retains, his high standing as an authority on these subjects being generally recognized. He first entered the political field in a by-election for the Local House in 1888, and was defeated. Ran again at the provincial general elections in 1890, and was again defeated. Was finally returned at general elections in 1896. A Liberal.—*Ste. Rose, Q.*

ODILON DESMARAIS,

(St. James Division, Montreal.)

Odilon Desmarais was born in Joliette, February 28, 1854. His family emigrated from Normandy, France, one of whom was a son-in-law to Champlain. He was educated at the Joliette College and at McGill University, where he graduated a B.C.L. in March, 1876, getting at the same time the premium of thesis. In May, 1877, he married a sister of the late Mr. A. Gelinas, who was Editor of *La Minerve*. Mr. Desmarais has been President of several local societies, and was a Councillor of St. Hyacinthe for two years. He is by profession an advocate, and has for several years been a journalist. He represented St. Hyacinthe in the Legislative Assembly of Quebec from 1890 to 1892. He was first elected to the House of Commons at the general elections held in 1895. Practicing his profession in Montreal since 1892, he particularly distinguished himself as counsel for the defense in the celebrated murder case of Demers. He is actually Crown Prosecutor for the Montreal District. A Liberal.—*Montreal*.

DUNCAN GRAHAM.

(North Ontario.)

Duncan Graham was born in the Township of Thora, County of Ontario, Province of Ontario, on October 5, 1845. He is of Scotch descent, and is the son of Archibald Graham and Anne McQuaig, both of whom were natives of Islay, Scotland. He was educated in the Public Schools in the District of Thora. Mr. Graham's occupation is farming in all its branches. He has occupied several public offices, such as Councillor, Deputy Reeve and Reeve of Mara Township for a period of ten years, and was also Warden of the County of Ontario for 1896. He was first elected to the House of Commons for the North Riding of Ontario County at a by-election held in February, 1897. A Liberal-Independent. —*Gamebridge, O.*

LIEUT.-COL. JAMES DOMVILLE.

(Kings, N.B.)

James Domville, son of the late Lieut.-General James William Domville and Frances, daughter of Hon. Wm. Usher, was born on Nov. 29, 1842. He was educated in England. Married, in 1867, Isabel, daughter of the late Wm. H. Scovil, Esq., of St. John, N.B. Was at one time extensively engaged in iron manufacturing. Has been President of King's Co. Board of Trade. Is a Lieut.-Col. of the 8th Princess Louise Hussars. He was first elected to the House of Commons at the general elections 1872, defeated in 1882, and re-elected in 1896. A Liberal.—*The Willows, Rothesay, N.B.*

J. M. DOUGLAS.

(East Assiniboia.)

James Moffatt Douglas was born in Linton, Bankhead, Roxborough-shire, Scotland, on May 26, 1838. He was educated at the Parish School there, and at Toronto University and Knox College, Toronto, and afterwards graduated at the Theological Seminary, Princeton, N.J. In 1861 he married Jane, daughter of Mr. George Smith. Mr. Douglas has been a minister of the Presbyterian Church in Canada from 1867, and was also in pastoral charge at Uxbridge and Cobourg, Ont.,

Brandon, Man., and Moosomin, N.W.T. He was also, from 1876 to 1882, a pioneer missionary to Central India, and the Chaplain to Her Majesty's Troops at Mhow. He has taken an active part in the development of the North-West Territories, and of the Presbyterian Church in Manitoba. He was a member of the Ontario Board of Public Instruction, and was Inspector of the Common Schools in the Township of Uxbridge. He was Chairman of the High School Board, Cobourg, and was also President of the Cobourg Evangelical Alliance. He was first elected to Parliament at the general elections held in 1896. He is a Liberal, but was nominated by the Patrons of Industry as an Independent.—*Tantallon, Assa.*

W. C. EDWARDS.

(Russell.)

William Cameron Edwards was born in the Township of Clarence, Ont., in 1844, being a son of the late Wm. Edwards, of Portsmouth, Eng., who came to Canada about the year 1820. He was educated at the Ottawa Grammar School. He married in January, 1885, the eldest daughter of William Wilson, Esq., of Cumberland. Mr. Edwards is by occupation a lumber manufacturer. In 1882 he was an unsuccessful candidate for the seat he now holds. He was first elected to Parliament at the general election of 1887, but, his election being declared void, a new election was held on May 7, 1888, when he was re-elected. He was also re-elected at the general elections of 1891 and 1896. A Liberal.—*Rockland, O.*

P. M. GUAY, M.D.

(Levis.)

Pierre Malcolm Guay was born at St. Romuald d'Etchemin, March 26, 1848. He is a son of the late Francois Xavier Guay, his mother being Marie Adelaide Coté. His ancestors, who came from Saintonge, France, were among the first settlers of Pointe Levis. Dr. Guay was educated at the Quebec Seminary and at Laval University, at Quebec, where he graduated A. B. in 1868 and M.D. in 1872. He married, May 12, 1874, Marie Louise Antoinette Roy, daughter of the late T. E. Roy, formerly

Sergeant-at-Arms of the Legislative Council of Quebec, who died May 24, 1892. Dr. Guay, who has been practicing medicine and surgery in St. Romuald since 1872, has been a Governor of the College of Physicians and Surgeons of the Province of Quebec since 1883. He was also Municipal Councillor and Mayor of the village of St. Romuald d'Etchemin. He has been the Liberal Whip for the Province of Quebec since 1891. He was first returned to Parliament at the by-election held April 14, 1885, and was re-elected at the general elections of 1887, 1891 and 1896. A Liberal.—*Etchemin, Q.*

JOSEPH GODBOUT, M.D.

(Beauce.)

Joseph Godbout was born at St. Vital de Lambton, County of Beauce, and is the son of Joseph Godbout, farmer, who was a descendant of the pioneer settler in St. Vital de Lambton, County of Beauce. He was educated at Laval University and the Quebec Seminary. He graduated at Laval University in March, 1877, in medicine, and subsequently removed to St. Francois, where he has followed his profession ever since. He has been married twice; first on October 8, 1878, at Quebec, to Rachel Audet, who died January 21, 1881, and second to Mrs. G. N. Fauteux, née Hermine St. Pierre. He was elected Governor of the Bureau of Physicians for the Province of Quebec in July, 1895. He was first elected to Parliament at the general election of 1887, and re-elected at the general elections held in 1891 and 1896. A Liberal.—*St. Francois, Beauce, Q.*

JOHN FRASER.

(East Lambton.)

John Fraser was born in Inverness-shire, Scotland, March 3, 1849, and is the son of late Donald Fraser, of Inverness-shire, and Jane Noble, of Ross-shire, Scotland, who came to Canada in 1850. He was educated in the Public Schools, in the Middlesex Seminary and by private tuition. Mr. Fraser is engaged in the production of petroleum, and is a Director of the Petrolia Crude Oil & Tanking Co. He married on April 23, 1879, Ellen Harlow, daughter of James McGill, Esq., of Petrolia. He has been manager of the Crown Savings & Loan Co. during the past 10 years, and has been Councillor and four years Mayor of Petrolia. He has also been President of the Petrolia Club, Dufferin Club, Petrolia Literary Society, St. Andrew's Society, Shakespeare Club, and Chieftain of the Clan Fraser for the London District. He was first elected to the House of Commons at the general elections of 1896. A Liberal.—*Petrolia, O.*

A. E. DYMENT.

(Algoma.)

Albert Edward Dyment was born at Lynden, County of Wentworth, Ont., in 1869. He is of English and Scotch descent, being a son of Nathaniel Dyment, whose father, John Dyment, was a native of Devonshire, England, and his mother, Annie McRae, of Inverness-shire, Scotland. He was educated at Barrie Collegiate Institute, and later at the Upper Canada College. He was married June 1, 1892, to Edith F. Chapman, of Hamilton, daughter of the late A. J. Chapman, of London, Ont. He is by occupation a lumberman. He is the youngest member of the present House of Commons but one, and the first Liberal member returned from Algoma. He was elected a Councillor of Barrie at the age of 22. He was first elected to Parliament in June, 1896, when he defeated his opponent, Mr. G. H. MacDonnell, by a vote of 3,176 to 1,349, turning a former Conservative majority of 438 into a Liberal majority of 1827 A Liberal.—*Thessalon, O.*

DAVID HENDERSON.

(Halton.)

David Henderson was born in the Township of Nelson, Ont., February 18, 1841, and is the son of John Henderson, who in 1832 emigrated from Scotland, and settled in the Township of Nelson, Ont. He was educated at the Milton Grammar School, and at the Normal School, Toronto. Mr. Henderson is engaged in business as a general merchant. He married in 1865, Alison, daughter of Mr. Charles Christie. He has been a member of the Municipal Councils of Milton and Acton. In 1866 he was appointed Deputy Registrar of Deeds for the County of Halton, and continued so until 1873. He was first elected to the Commons at a by-election held in 1888, but his election was declared void. In 1891 he was re-elected, but was unseated, and in 1892 was again re-elected, also in 1896. A Conservative, and an ardent supporter of the N.P.—*Acton, O.*

J. A. C. ETHIER.

(Two Mountains.)

J. A. C. Ethier, the new member for Two Mountains, was born at St. Benoit, in the District which he represents in the House, on May 26, 1868. His father is J. Bte. Ethier, a successful and highly esteemed farmer of St. Benoit. Mr. Ethier was educated at Montreal College, and afterwards studied law, being admitted to the Bar in January, 1895. Previous to that date he acted as Deputy Prothonotary of the Superior Court for the District of Terrebonne, at St. Scholastique, from 1888 to 1895, and it was at that place that he prosecuted his legal studies under Hon. Wilfred Prevost, C.R. Though but a short time in the actual practice of his profession, Mr. Ethier's thorough experience and long preliminary training have given him an amount of knowledge of the literature and practical methods of the law which give him an assured standing in his profession. He is a ready debater, an acute reasoner, and will undoubtedly justify the choice of his constituents. He was married in April, 1889, to Therese Fortier, daughter of Dr. L. A. Fortier, of St. Scholastique, and was elected to represent Two Mountains at the last general elections. A Liberal.—*Ste. Scholastique, Q.*

CHARLES B. HEYD.

(South Brant.)

Charles Bernhard Heyd was born in Rochester, N.Y., February 23, 1842, his father being a native of Switzerland, and his mother a Prussian. He received his early education in Rochester, but afterwards attended school at Brantford. He is a merchant by occupation, and for five years filled the office of Alderman of that city. He has also been Mayor for three years and a half, and Water Commissioner for ten years. He was elected to his present seat at the by-election held February 4, 1897. At the general elections of 1896 Robert Henry (Conservative) was elected, but his election was voided. A Liberal.—*Brantford, O.*

D. K. ERB.

(South Perth.)

Dilman Kinsey Erb, who represents South Perth in the new Parliament, is of Pennsylvania-Dutch descent and was born in the County of Waterloo, Ont., in 1857. He was educated at the Public Schools of his native place, and taught school eight years. He has been School Trustee for nine years, and has always taken a lively interest in the promotion of education within the sphere of his influence. For four years he was President of the Sebringville Flax Co., Ltd., and took much interest in the development of the growth of that crop in the district. He was Township Councillor for two years and Deputy Reeve for three years. He is highly respected for his business ability and straightforwardness in all his transactions, and has always been a thorough-going Liberal in politics, and will always be found ready to support every measure which commends itself to his judgment as being for the best interests of the country. He was elected to the Dominion House at the last general elections for the first time. A Liberal.—*Sebringville, O.*

H. S. HARWOOD.

(Vaudreuil.)

Henry Stanislaus Harwood was born in Vaudreuil, P.Q., August 8, 1840, and is the fifth son of the late Hon. Robert Unwin Harwood, a native of Sheffield, Eng., who represented the Rigaud division in the Legislative Council of Canada until his death in 1863, his mother being a daughter of the late Hon. Alain Chartier de Lotbinière, Seigneur of Vaudreuil, de Lotbinière and Rigaud, and granddaughter of the Marquis de Lotbinière. He was educated at St. Mary's College, Montreal, and is by profession Provincial Land Surveyor. He married, May 17, 1864, Josephine Sidney, daughter of the late J. C. Brauneis, Esq. Was first returned to Parliament at the general elections of 1891 ; was unseated, but re-elected in 1893. Re-elected at the general elections of 1896.— *Vaudreuil, Q.*

J. V. ELLIS.

(St. John City.)

John Valentine Ellis was born in Halifax, N.S., in 1835, of Irish parents. He moved to Montreal in 1854, and was resident there for about three years, returning again to the Lower Provinces, this time locating in St. John, N.B. He married in 1864, at Fredericton, N.B., a daughter of the late Samuel Babbitt, Esq. He is a journalist by profession, being editor of the St. John *Daily Globe*. He held the appointment of postmaster of St. John for a short period. Was a member of the New Brunswick Assembly from 1882 until January, 1887, when he resigned to contest his present seat for the Commons at the general elections of that year, in which he was successful. Defeated in 1891, he was re-elected in 1896. Mr. Ellis is well known throughout Canada in connection with the Queen's, N.B. election in 1887, having been condemned by the Supreme Court of New Brunswick to pay a fine of $200 and undergo imprisonment for one month for contempt of court through his criticisms affecting a judgment rendered in connection with the election in that County by Judge Tuck. Mr. Ellis' friends all over Canada raised two thousand dollars and paid the greater part of his expenses. A Liberal.—*St. John, N.B.*

W. T. HODGINS.

(Carleton, Ont.)

William Thomas Hodgins was born in the Township of Goulburn, February 27, 1857. He is the son of the late Mr. John Hodgins, and a grandson of Mr. William Hodgins, a native of Tipperary, Ireland, who was one of the pioneer settlers in Carleton Co., Ont. He was educated at the Common School at Goulburn. He is by occupation a farmer. In 1888 he was a member of Municipal Council of the Township of Goulburn. First returned to the House of Commons at the general election in 1891, and re-elected in 1896. A Conservative.—*Hazeldean, O.*

HERCULE DUPRE.

(St. Mary's Division, Montreal.)

Hercule Dupré was born in the year 1842 at Vercheres, Vercheres Co., Que., his father being the late Captain Pierre Dupré, a wealthy farmer, whose family is one of the oldest in the County. Mr. Dupré was educated at the Parish School, and remained on his father's farm until he was about 28 years of age, when he left his native place and settled in Montreal, starting in the lumber business in company with Mr. Chaussé, doing a prosperous business. After four years a third member was added to the firm, which became known as Chaussé, Dupré & Cie., continuing so for eight years. Retiring from the business, Mr. Dupré formed a partnership with his brother as Dupré & Frères, lumber merchants, which continued prosperously until 1891, when his brother retired and he continued alone. In 1862 he was married to Mlle. Vitaline Giard, of Contrecœur, Que. He has taken a deep interest in municipal affairs almost since his settlement in Montreal, and in 1894 was chosen by the electors of St. Mary's Ward to represent them in the City Council, being returned by a majority of 434. First returned to Parliament at the general elections of 1896 defeating his opponent by a majority of 1,363 votes. A Liberal.—*Montreal.*

CHRISTIAN KLOEPFER.

(South Wellington.)

Christian Kloepfer was born in New Germany, County of Waterloo, Ont., December 22, 1847, and is of German descent, his parents having emigrated from Baden, Germany, to Canada about 1842. He was educated at the Parochial School in New Germany. Mr. Kloepfer is in business as a wholesale carriage hardware merchant. He married in June, 1880, Elizabeth Murphy, of Guelph. He is a director of several trading institutions, and has been an alderman of Guelph. He was first elected to the House of Commons at the general elections held in 1896. A Liberal-Conservative.—*Guelph, O.*

JOSEPH FEATHERSTON.
(Peel.)

Joseph Featherston was born in the Township of Trafalgar, County of Halton, July 22, 1843, his father being a native of Durham County, Eng., and his mother of Ireland. He was educated in the County. He married February 6, 1867, Isabella, daughter of John Malloy, of the Township of Vaughan. Mr. Featherston is a farmer, and is also a breeder and dealer in thoroughbred stock. He has held the offices of a Municipal Councillor, Deputy Reeve and Reeve. In 1887 he was President of the Dominion Live Stock Association, and was also first Vice-President of the Dominion Live Stock Insurance Co. in 1887-1888, and in 1890 and 1891 was President of the Canadian Swine Breeders' Association. First returned to Parliament at the general elections of 1891, but, his election being declared void, he was re-elected at a by-election held February 11, 1892. Re-elected at the general elections held in 1896. A Liberal.—*Streetsville, O*

FREDERIC HARDINGE HALE.
(Carleton, N.B.)

Frederic Hardinge Hale was born at Northampton, Carleton Co., N.B., December 8, 1844. Fourth son of Martin Hale, who (with his brother, who was the proprietor of a wholesale clothing store in St. John, N.B.) emigrated to New Brunswick from the North of Ireland in 1815. Martin Hale settled in the Parish of Northampton, and married Hilda Dickinson, the daughter of Hardinge Dickinson, a U. E. Loyalist. Mr. Hale has been in business as a lumber merchant for twentyfive years. He married first, Rhoda, daughter of George McGee, Esq.; second, Emma E., daughter of Moses Boyer, Esq.; third, Lina N., daughter of J. Faulkner, of King's County, N.B. Mr. Hale was first elected to Parliament at the general election in 1887, and sat until the dissolution in 1891. He declined nomination in 1891. He was a candidate, and elected at the general election in 1896. A Liberal-Conservative.—*Woodstock, N.B.*

WILLIAM GIBSON.

(Lincoln & Niagara.)

William Gibson was born at Peterhead, Scotland, August 7, 1849, being the eldest son of the late Mr. Wm. Gibson, ship builder there. He was educated at the Peterhead Academy. Was married in 1876 to Jennie Hill, eldest daughter of the late Mr. John F. Davidson, merchant, Hamilton, Ont. He came to Canada in 1870 and entered the service of the old Great Western Railway. Is an Associate Member of the Canadian Society of Civil Engineers, and a Railway Contractor, having been engaged on a large number of important Public Works, chief among which was the masonry work of both ends of the St. Clair Tunnel, also the enlargement of the New Welland Canal on Section J, near Thorold, Ontario. For the past twenty years he has built the masonry of all the principal structures on the Grand Trunk Railway west of Toronto, and at present is engaged in building the masonry of the new and enlarged Victoria Bridge, Montreal. In addition to his being a Railway Contractor, he owns and operates two of the most extensive limestone quarries in Canada near Beamsville, and at Crookston. He is President of the Hamilton Street Ry. and a Director of the Bank of Hamilton, The Hamilton Provident & Loan Society, The Hamilton Gas Light Company, The Keewatin Power Company, Norman, Ont., and the Keewatin Lumbering and Manufacturing Co., Keewatin, Ontario. He is also a Director of the Presbyterian Ladies' College, Toronto. Takes a great interest in Freemasonry, and is Grand Master of the Grand Lodge of Canada. Was first returned to Parliament in 1891. Unseated on petition; re-elected with a largely increased majority at by-election the following year, and again at the general elections of 1896. Is Liberal whip for the Province of Ontario in the Dominion House of Commons and Chairman of the Joint Committee on Printing of both Houses of Parliament.—*Beamsville, O.*

HON. J. G. HAGGART.

(South Lanark.)

The Hon. John Graham Haggart was born in Perth, Ont., November 14, 1836. He is the son of John Haggart, Esq., formerly of Breadalbane, Perthshire, Scotland, and afterwards of Perth, Lanark, Ont., and Isabella Graham of Isle of Skye, Inverness-shire, Scotland. He was Mayor of Perth for several years At the general elections of 1867 and 1869 he was a candidate for South Lanark in the Legislative Assembly of Ontario, but was defeated. He was first elected to Parliament in 1872, and was re-elected in 1874, 1878, 1882, 1887, 1891 and 1896. In August, 1888, he was sworn of the Privy Council, and appointed Postmaster-General, and held office until January, 1892, when he received the appointment of Minister of Railways and Canals. He has been a member of the Macdonald, Abbott, Thompson, Bowell and Tupper Administrations, and retired with the latter Administration in July, 1896. A Liberal-Conservative.—*Perth, O.*

A. B. INGRAM.

(East Elgin.)

Andrew B. Ingram was born at Strabane, County of Wentworth, April 23, 1851, and is the second son of the late Thomas Ingram of Quebec. His grandfather was a native of Tyrone, Ireland, and served nineteen years in the British Army under the Duke of Wellington, and afterwards removed to the County of Halton, Ont. He was educated at Morristown and Aberfoyle, Ont. He held a seat in the Legislative Assembly of Ontario for West Elgin from 1886 until 1890. In June, 1882, he married Elizabeth, daughter of Mr. Allen McIntyre, of Aberfoyle. He was first elected to the House of Commons in 1891, but his election was declared void, and a by-election was held in February, 1892, when he was re-elected. He was also re-elected at the general elections of 1896. A Liberal-Conservative.—*St. Thomas, O.*

D. C. FRASER.

(Guysborough.)

Duncan Cameron Fraser was born in the County of Pictou, N.S., October 1, 1845. He is of Scottish descent, his grandparents coming from Inverness, Scotland. He was educated at Dalhousie College, Halifax, from whence he graduated in 1872. In October, 1878, he was married to a daughter of Wm. Graham, Esq., of New Glasgow. Studied law and was admitted to the Bar of Nova Scotia in 1873. Has been twice Mayor of New Glasgow, and several times President of the Alumni of Dalhousie College. Mr. Fraser is a prominent Freemason, and was Grand Master of the Grand Lodge of Nova Scotia. In 1878 he was a member of the Legislative Council of that province and of the Hill Administration, but resigned the same year. In 1887 was reappointed to the Council, and became a member of the Executive without portfolio, and was Leader of the Government in the Legislative Council from 1887 to 1891, when he resigned to run for the Commons. He was successful, and was re-elected at the general elections of 1896. A Liberal.—*New Glasgow, N.S.*

GEORGE McHUGH.

(South Victoria, Ont.)

George McHugh was born in the Township of Ops, County of Victoria, July 7, 1845, and is the 3rd son of the late Patrick McHugh and Anne Walker, who emigrated from Ireland. He is a grandson of Sergt. Roger McHugh, who served under Wellington. He was educated at the common schools in the vicinity. He is by occupation a farmer. He was married in Peterborough, February 25, 1873, to Margaret, only daughter of the late James O'Neill. He held the office of President of the Reform Association of South and West Victoria, and was also a Member of the Ontario Executive Reform Association. He was first elected to the House of Commons at the general elections held in 1896. A Liberal.—*Lindsay. O.*

C. A. GAUVREAU.
(Temiscouata.)

Charles Arthur Gauvreau was born at St. Jean Baptiste, Isle Verte, County of Temiscouata, September 29, 1860, his father being L. N. Gauvreau, Esq., N.P. He is the Seigneur of the manor of that name, and nephew of the late Sir N. F. Belleau, first Lieut.-Governor of the Province of Quebec. He was educated at the College of Rimouski, where he took the degree of A.B., and at Laval University, Quebec. He is a notary by profession, and studied law in the office of Messrs. Laurier, Lavergne & Coté. Mr. Gauvreau is a Commissioner of the Superior Court, also Commissioner for the Decision of Small Cases, and Recording Secretary of L'Alliance National of Princeville, also holding the office of Secretary-Treasurer for the Municipal Council of St. Norbert, Arthabaska. He is the author of several works, among which are "The History of Isle Verte," "The History of Trois Pistoles." He also published two Canadian stories, "Captive et Bourreau," "Les Epreuves d'un Orphelin." First elected to Parliament by acclamation at the by-election held in the latter part of 1897, owing to the death of Charles Eugène Pouliot, the sitting member. A Liberal.—*Stanfold, Q.*

J. F. LISTER, Q.C.
(West Lambton.)

James Frederick Lister was born at Belleville, Ont., June 21, 1843, and is the eldest son of Mr. George Lister, fifth son of Captain James Lister of the British Revenue Service. He was educated at the Sarnia Grammar School. Mr. Lister formerly studied law with his uncle, Mr. F. Davis, Judge of Middlesex County, and was admitted as an Attorney in September, 1865. Was called to the Bar of Ontario in 1875, and was appointed Q.C. by the Ontario Government in 1890. He has held the office

of Crown Prosecutor at the assizes for several years. He was first elected to the House of Commons at the general election held in 1882, and was re-elected at those of 1887, 1891 and 1895. A Liberal.—*Sarnia, O.*

J. A. GILLIES, M.A., Q.C.
(Richmond, N.S.)

Joseph Alexander Gillies was born at Irish Cove, Red Islands, Cape Breton, September 17, 1849. He is the third son of the late John Gillies, of Inverness shire, Scotland, and Mary McLean, of Coll, Argyleshire. He was educated at St. Francois Xavier's College, Antigonish, N.S., graduating an M.A. in 1870. In 1875 he was called to the Bar of Nova Scotia, and was Clerk of the Peace for Cape Breton for some years, and afterwards held the same office for the Municipality, which he resigned, and is now Solicitor for the latter Corporation. In 1872 he was appointed Registrar of Probate for the County, and held that position until Febry., 1887, when he resigned. He married in July, 1883, Josephine Eulalie, daughter of Seraphin Bertrand, of Prescott, Ont. In 1887 he was a candidate for Cape Breton, but was defeated. He was first elected to Parliament in 1891, but the election being declared void, he was re-elected in January, 1892, at a by-election, and was re-elected in 1896. Was created Queen's Counsel by the Dominion Government in 1895. A strong advocate of Imperial Federation and in the closest possible unification of the British Empire. A Liberal-Conservative.—*Sydney, Cape Breton, N.S.*

H. J. LOGAN.
(Cumberland.)

Hance James Logan was born at Amherst Point, N.S., April 26, 1869, and is the son of James Archibald Logan. His mother was a daughter of Hance B. Hunter, of Scottish descent, and who was a leading Justice of Cumberland. He was educated at the Model School, Truro, the Pictou Academy, and at Dalhousie University, from which institution he graduated in 1891 as a Bachelor of Laws. Mr. Logan is at present a practising barrister of Nova Scotia. He married in 1891 Eleanor L. Kinder. He was first elected to the House of Commons at the general election held in 1896. A Liberal.—*Amherst, N.S.*

JAMES GILMOUR.

(East Middlesex.)

James Gilmour is one of the new members, having been returned to Parliament for the first time at the last general elections. He was born on the farm of South Hillhead, Mearns, Renfrewshire, Scotland, whence he and his relatives emigrated to Canada in 1861, and settled in the County where they still reside. Mr. Gilmour received the solid and thorough education which is to be obtained at all Scotch schools at the Public School of his native place. During his public career in this country he has been Councillor, Deputy Reeve, Reeve and Warden of his County, and Hospital Trustee of the General Hospital, London, Ont., and is a Justice of the Peace in the County of Middlesex, all of which goes to show how thorough is the confidence which his friends who know him best repose in his sterling character and ability. He is still Reeve of his County, having been elected 13 times by acclamation and without any show of opposition. Is a practical business man who will always weigh and discuss every public question on its merits. He is a farmer and a very skillful and successful one. He is married to Sarah Elizabeth McClary, of Westminster Township, eldest daughter of Peter McClary, Esq., J.P., Collector of Inland Revenue, London. A Conservative.—*Nilestown, O.*

T. MACKIE.

(North Renfrew.)

Thomas Mackie was born in the city of Ottawa, and is of Scottish descent. He was educated in the city of Ottawa. Mr. Mackie is engaged in business as a lumber merchant. He married Miss Jessie Shaw, of Lake Doré, County of Renfrew. He has held a seat as a member of the Pembroke Town Council. He was first elected to the House of Commons at the general elections held in 1896, when he defeated the Hon. P. White, the Conservative candidate, by a vote of 1,900 to 1,837. A Liberal.—*Pembroke, O.*

J. LIVINGSTON.

(South Waterloo.)

James Livingston was born in East Kilbride. Scotland, November 29, 1838. He was educated at the same place, and came to Canada in 1856. Mr. Livingston is a merchant, but has for several years been largely interested in the cultivation of flax and the manufacturing of linseed oil. He married in June, 1861, Miss Louisa Liersch of Baden. He has been Reeve of the Township of Wilmot. In 1879 he was elected to the Legislative Assembly of Ontario for South Waterloo, and resigned in May, 1882. At the general election of 1882 he was first elected to the House of Commons, and was re-elected at the general elections of 1887, 1891 and 1896. A Reformer.—*Baden, O.*

A. C. MACDONALD.

(Kings, P.E.I.)

Augustine Colin Macdonald was born at Panmure, P.E.I., June 30, 1837, being a son of Hugh and Catherine Macdonald, who came to Prince Edward Island in 1805, from Moydart, Inverness-shire, Scotland. He was educated at Georgetown Grammar School and the Central Academy at Charlottetown. Mr. Macdonald is a merchant, and has been a Commissioner for managing the Exhibition of Local Industry for Prince Edward Island at various times, and also holds the rank of Captain in the Militia. His first Parliamentary experience was in 1870, when he became a member of the P.E.I. House of Assembly, representing the 3rd District of Kings County until July 1, 1873, when Prince Edward Island entered the Dominion. He was first elected to the Canadian Parliament at the general elections of 1873, was defeated in 1874, re-elected in 1878 and 1882, defeated in 1887 and re-elected in 1891 and 1896. He married June 27, 1865, Mary Elizabeth, sixth daughter of the late Hon. John Small Macdonald. In favor of preferential trade with Great Britain and the other colonies on fair terms. A Liberal-Conservative.—*Montague Bridge, P.E.I.*

GEORGE GUILLET.

(West Northumberland.)

George Guillet was born in Cobourg, Ont., in 1840, his father being a native of the Island of Jersey, and his mother an English lady. He was educated at the Public School of Cobourg and at Victoria College. He is a prominent merchant of that town; for several years was a member of the Town Council, and for four years acted as Mayor; on his retirement was offered re-election by acclamation. He was an unsuccessful candidate for his present seat in the Legislative Assembly of Ontario in 1879, but was returned to Parliament December 19, 1881; re-elected in 1882 and unseated by a judgment of the Supreme Court, March 17, 1885; re-elected April 7, 1885, and again at the general elections of 1887; unsuccessful in 1891, at the general elections, which was voided; he was successful at the by-election held on March 15, 1892, and re-elected at the general elections of 1896. Was instrumental in obtaining the extension of the clauses of the Merchants' Shipping Act of 1873 to the inland waters of Canada, which secures to seamen a first lien and the right of recovery of wages in rem and by summary process.—*Cobourg, O.*

P. MACDONALD, M.D.

(East Huron.)

Peter Macdonald was born in Pictou, N. S., August 14, 1835. He is of Scotch descent, his parents having come from Inverness, Scotland, in 1830 to Pictou, and in 1846 they removed to the County of Huron. He was educated in Toronto. Mr. Macdonald is by profession a practising physician. He married in February, 1866, Miss Margaret Ross. He has held the position of Chairman of the Board of School Trustees for several years, and has been Reeve, Councillor and Mayor of the town of Wingham. He was first elected to the House of Commons at the general elections of 1887, and was re-elected at those of 1891 and 1896, A Liberal.—*Wingham, O.*

ALLEN HALEY.

(Hants.)

Allen Haley was born January 31, 1844, in Yarmouth, N.S., of mixed Irish and Scotch parentage. He was educated at the Yarmouth Academy, and at private schools, afterwards studying medicine, and graduated in 1866 from the Dental College, Philadelphia, Pa. Mr. Haley is now engaged as an insurance agent and broker, and among the public offices he holds is that of Secretary of the Shipowners' Marine, of Windsor, N.S., Director Nova Scotia Telephone Co., Halifax Electric Tram Co., and other local companies; Manager and Owner of Merchant Shipping. He first entered public life as a member of the Nova Scotia Assembly in 1882, was re-elected in 1886 and 1890, resigned in 1891, and stood for the House of Commons, but was defeated. At the general elections in 1896 he again contested the seat, and was elected as a supporter of the present Administration. Mr. Haley is a believer in national progress, and the advancement of Canada and Canadian Institutions, a warm supporter of British connection and opposed to chimerical independence or annexation to the United States. A Liberal.—*Windsor, N.S.*

J. H. LEGRIS.

(Maskinongé.)

Joseph Hormidas Legris was born at Rivière du Loup (en haut). He was educated by private tuition and at the Model School in the Parish of Louiseville. Mr. Legris is by occupation a farmer. He married in June, 1879, Emma, daughter of George Champagne, of Berthier. He was the organizer of a Mutual Fire Insurance Co., and held the position of Secretary. He has also been a Captain in the 86th Batt. Volunteer Militia. He occupied a seat in the Legislative Assembly of Quebec from April, 1888, until 1890. He is Secretary-Treasurer of the Parish. At the general elections of 1891 he was first elected to the House of Commons, and was re-elected at that of 1896. A Liberal—*Louiseville, Q.*

MAJOR SAMUEL HUGHES.

(North Victoria.)

Major Hughes is a native of Durham County, near Bowmanville, Ont., and is in his forty-fifth year. He was educated in the Provincial Model and Normal Schools of Ontario in Toronto, the University of Toronto, from which he holds honor certificates in English, French, German and history, and in the Military School under the 29th Regiment of the Line. Began teaching in Belleville when only 16 years of age, and subsequently was head of Lifford and Bowmanville Public Schools. For ten years—1875 to 1885—Mr. Hughes was in Toronto Collegiate Institute as first English master. He is intensely energetic; besides being proprietor of the Victoria *Warder* and largely connected with several important business enterprises, he yet finds time to devote to his military duties as major of the 45th Battalion. In politics Major Hughes is a Liberal-Conservative and favors preferential trade among Great Britain and her colonies, and ultimately of the English-speaking race.

JOHN LANG.

(Peterborough East.)

John Lang was born in the Village Keene, April 10, 1839, and is the son of James Lang and Agnes Stewart, both of Renfrewshire, Scotland, who removed to Canada in 1832 and 1820 respectively. Was educated at the Common School in Keene. In November, 1866, he married Elizabeth Shearer. Was appointed J.P. in 1870, was elected to the Otonabee Township Council in 1872, which seat he held continuously for 16 years, and for 13 years held the Reeve and Deputy Reeveship, and there never was a ballot printed for him, being elected every time by acclamation. He was first elected to the House of Commons at the general elections of 1887; he resigned the Reeveship next year, and did not offer for re-election at the general elections in 1891, and was again re-elected in 1896. An Independent-Liberal.—*Jermyn, O.*

J. M. HURLEY.

(East Riding of Hastings.)

Jeremiah M. Hurley was born near Picton, Prince Edward County, Ont., in 1840, of Irish parentage, and was educated at the public school of the County of Hastings. He is a highly successful farmer and breeder of live stock, his specialties being carriage horses, trotters and hogs (improved Yorkshires), of which latter he is also an extensive shipper. Has been expert judge on horses and swine at some of the leading Fairs in Ontario, viz., Toronto Industrial and Guelph fat stock show, Kingston, etc. Mr. Hurley was appointed a J.P. in 1876; has been a member of the County Council of Hastings for over twelve years; chairman of the Roads and Bridges Committee; President and Director of the Thurlow Cheese Factory; ex-President of the Cheese Board of Trade of Belleville; Director of the Farmers' Institute; member of the Breeders' Association and Manager and Secretary of the Bay of Quinté Exhibition for several years. For many years Mr. Hurley has taken an active part in every movement tending to promote the interests of agriculture, and it was probably owing to this well-known characteristic that he secured his seat in the present parliament. A Liberal.—*Belleville, O.*

G. LANDERKIN, M.D.

(South Grey.)

George Landerkin was born at West Gwillimbury, Simcoe, in 1839, and is the son of the late James Landerkin, Esq., formerly of Nova Scotia, and who afterwards settled in the County of Simcoe in 1824. He was educated at the Victoria College, Cobourg, from which institution he graduated an M.D. in 1862. He married, in 1870, Miss M. Kirkendall, of Elora, Ont. Mr. Landerkin was first elected to the House of Commons at the general elections of 1872, and was re-elected in 1874. At the general elections of 1878 he was defeated, but was re-elected at the general elections of 1882, 1887, 1891 and 1896. A Liberal.—*Hanover, O.*

R. W. JAMESON.
(Winnipeg.)

R. W. Jameson was born at Cape Town, in the Cape of Good Hope, July 12, 1851, and is a son of the late Lieut.-Gen. Sir George Jameson, K.C.S.I. On the return of his parents to England in 1857, they became resident at Blackheath, near London, and at the Proprietary School there Mr. Jameson received his early education. He afterwards attended King's College, London, and Trinity College, Cambridge, where he graduated with the degree of B.A. Was called to the Bar of England in 1876, when 25 years of age, and the same year he came to Canada, where he served articles with the firm of Rose, Macdonald & Merritt, of Toronto. Mr. Jameson was subsequently admitted to the Ontario Bar, and practiced in Toronto in 1881. In that year the Manitoba boom was at its height, and Mr. Jameson went to Winnipeg. In 1882 he was admitted to the Manitoba Bar. Mr. Jameson's first public office was that of License Commissioner, to which he was appointed on the creation of that Board in 1890. Elected Alderman in 1892; he resigned in 1895 to accept nomination of the Mayoralty, to which office he was elected. Returned to Parliament at by-election in 1897.—*Winnipeg, Man.*

J. B. KLOCK.
(Nipissing.)

James Bell Klock was born at Aylmer, Que., October 5, 1856, and is the eldest son of the late Robert H. Klock, who was one of the pioneer lumbermen of the Ottawa Valley. He was educated at the Aylmer Academy and at Berthier. Is engaged in business as a lumberman, farmer and stock raiser. He married in December, 1883, Alice, daughter of the late Hon. Wm. McDougall, Judge of the Superior Court. He has held several public offices, such as President of the Agricultural and Art Association of Nipissing and Reeve of the Township of Cameron. First elected to the Commons in 1896. A Conservative.—*Klock's Mills, O.*

J. A. MACDONELL.
(Selkirk.)

John Alexander Macdonell was born at Dundas, County of Wentworth, Ont., on November 22, 1854. He was educated in Hamilton, and later at the Model School and School of Technology and Practical Science, Toronto. He is now a member of the Canadian Society of Engineers, and has been employed on various public and railway works. He also built a large portion of the heavy embankment across the Pembina River Valley. Was Chief Clerk of the Public Works Department in Manitoba, and is now the Chief Engineer of that Province. Sat in the Legislative Assembly of Manitoba, for Lorne, from the general elections of 1886 to 1888, when he was defeated. Was first returned to Parliament at the general elections of 1896. A Liberal.—*Winnipeg, Man.*

LIEUT.-COL. C. E. KAULBACH.
(Lunenburg.)

Lieut-Col. Charles Edwin Kaulbach was born at Lunenburg, July 13, 1834. He is of German descent, and is the son of Lieut.-Col. J. H. Kaulbach, High Sheriff of Lunenburg, N.S. He was educated at Lunenburg. Mr. Kaulbach is Vice-President of the Ottawa Board of Mercy; of the Nova Scotia Society for the Prevention of Cruelty to Animals; is Lieut-Col. of the 75th Batt. Volunteer Militia, and a Director of the Lunenburg Marine Insurance Co. and of the Lunenburg Marine Ship Co., Limited. He is a real estate and ship owner. At the general elections of 1878 he was first elected to the Commons, and was re-elected at that of 1882, but was deprived of his seat owing to the irregularity of two of the Deputy Returning Officers. His opponent held the seat for a year, and at the end of that time the seat was declared vacant by the Court, and in October, 1883, a new election was held in which he was re-elected. In 1887 he was defeated, but was re-elected in 1891 and 1896. A Conservative.—*Lunenburg, N.S.*

WILLIAM HUTCHISON.

(Ottawa City.)

William Hutchison was born in New Edinburgh in 1843, his father being the late Robert Hutchison, of Ayrshire, Scotland, who came to Canada about 1830. He was educated in his native place, and entered the flour milling business, in the prosecution of which he spent several years in the United States. Returning to Canada he went into business with his uncle, the late Thomas McKay, which later on was turned into a joint stock concern under the designation of the McKay Milling Co., of which Mr. Hutchison is now managing director. He was a member of the Ottawa City Council for a number of years, and Chairman of the Board of Works for four years; Director of the Chaudière Electric Light Co. and the Ottawa Electric Railway Co. and the Ottawa Land Association. He has also been Director for several years of the Central Canada Exhibition, and at present is its President. He is married to Electa Blanche, a daughter of S. T. Willett, Esq., of Chambly. Was first returned to Parliament at the general elections of 1896.—*Ottawa*.

T. H. MACPHERSON.

(Hamilton.)

Thomas Henry Macpherson was born in Perth, Scotland, in June, 1842, and was educated there and in London. He received his early business training on the Stock Exchange with the house of Messrs. Borthwick & Co., London, Eng., an experience which has since been of much service to him during his business career. Coming to Canada in 1871, he entered the firm of Alex. Harvey & Co., and subsequently became senior member of the well-known grocery firm of Macpherson, Glassco & Co., of Hamilton.

Among the public offices held by him is that of President of the Hamilton Board of Trade and President of the Liberal Association of Hamilton. He was first returned to Parliament at the general elections of 1896. A Liberal.—*Hamilton, O.*

RODOLPHE LEMIEUX.

(Gaspé.)

Rodolphe Lemieux was born in Montreal, November 1, 1866. His ancestors came from Normandy, France, and he is the son of H. A. Lemieux, formerly Collector of Customs at Three Rivers. He was educated at Nicolet and at Ottawa University. He is an Advocate by profession. He was admitted to the Bar of the Province of Quebec in 1892, and received the degree of Doctor of Law in Laval University, May 1, 1896. He was married on May 15, 1894, to Berthe, eldest daughter of the Hon. Mr. Justice Jetté. He is Consul for the United States of Colombia. He was Assistant Editor of *La Patrie* in 1886 and 1887, and was also correspondent of *L'Electeur* from 1887 until 1892. He was first elected to the House of Commons at the general election held in 1896 by defeating Mr. Thomas Ennis, Conservative. A Liberal.—*Montreal, Q.*

W. F. MACLEAN.

(East York.)

William Findlay Maclean was born in the Township of Ancaster, Ont., August 10, 1854, and is the son of John Maclean, a prominent newspaper writer of Canada. He was educated at the Hamilton public schools and at the University of Toronto, where he graduated a B. A. in 1880. Mr. Maclean is a journalist, and is proprietor of the *Toronto World*. He married in June, 1885, Catherine Gwynne, youngest daughter of Richard Lewis, of Toronto. He was a Member of the Senate of the University of Toronto for term of 1889 and 1892. At the general election of 1890 he ran for North Wentworth in the Ontario Legislature, but was defeated, and was also defeated for his present seat in the Commons at the general elections in 1891. At a by-election held in May, 1892, he was first elected to the Commons, and occupied the seat rendered vacant by the death of the Hon. A. Mackenzie, and was re-elected in 1896. A Conservative.—*Toronto, O.*

HON. W. B. IVES, Q.C.
(Sherbrooke.)

Hon. William Bullock Ives was born in the Township of Compton, P.Q., November 17, 1841. His parents were Eli Ives and Artimissa Bullock, both of English extraction, whose ancestors first settled in Connecticut. They moved to the County of Stanstead, P.Q., and were among the first settlers on Lake Memphremagog. Mr. Ives was partly educated in Compton Academy. Studied law, and was called to the Bar of the Province of Quebec in 1867. Married in 1869 the only daughter of the late Hon. J. H. Pope, Minister of Railways. Becoming largely interested in manufacturing, he gave up the practice of law in 1890. He represented Richmond and Wolfe in the Commons from the general elections of 1878 to the general elections of 1891, when he was returned for his present seat. Sworn of the Privy Council and appointed President of the Council December 6, 1892, and became Minister of Trade and Commerce, December 21, 1894. He was re-elected by acclamation at the general elections of 1896. Was a member of the Thompson, Bowell and Tupper Administrations, and resigned with his leader, July, 1896. A Conservative.—*Sherbrooke, Q.*

J. McALISTER.
(Restigouche.)

John McAlister was born in the Parish of Durham, Restigouche, July 27, 1842. He is of Scotch descent, his father having emigrated from Scotland to Canada, and settled in Restigouche in 1836. He was educated at the Common Schools there and at the Presbyterian Academy at Miramichi. In 1879 he was called to the Bar of New Brunswick, and was appointed a Q.C. in October, 1894. He is unmarried. Mr. McAlister was the first Mayor of the town of Campbellton. He was first elected to the House of Commons at the general elections held in 1891, and was re-elected at the general elections of 1896. A Liberal-Conservative.—*Campbellton, N.B.*

T. B. FLINT,
(Yarmouth.)

Thomas Barnard Flint was born in Yarmouth, N. S., April 28, 1847, being the son of John Flint, whose ancestors originally came from New England about 1761, and who with his maternal ancestors, the Barnards, were among the earliest settlers of the western part of Nova Scotia. He was educated at Yarmouth and at the Wesleyan Academy and College at Sackville, N.B., where he took his B.A. degree in 1867. In 1871 he graduated an LL.B. at Harvard University, Mass., and in 1872 graduated an M.A. at the Wesleyan College, Sackville, N.B. He was married in 1874 to Mary E., daughter of the late Thomas B. Dane, of Yarmouth. He is by profession a Barrister. From 1883 until 1886 he held the office of High Sheriff of Yarmouth County, and that of Assistant Clerk of the House of Assembly of N.S. from 1887 until 1890. He was an unsuccessful candidate for the House of Assembly for Yarmouth County at the general elections held in 1873 and 1882, and also for the House of Commons at the general election of 1878. He was first elected to Parliament at the general election held in 1881, and was re-elected at the general election of 1887. Mr. Flint has been prominently identified with Educational and Temperance work in the County of Yarmouth, and closely identified with its varied business interests since 1868. A Liberal.—*Yarmouth, N.S.*

A. MALOUIN.
(Quebec Centre.)

Albert Malouin was born in Quebec City, March 13, 1857, and is the son of Jacques Malouin, advocate and ex-member for Quebec Centre. He was educated at the Universities of Quebec and Laval, and is an advocate by profession, being admitted to the Bar in January, 1882. He is a member of the Council of the Quebec Bar, and Crown Prosecutor for the District of Quebec. He was elected to the House of Commons in January, 1898. A Liberal.—*Quebec.*

J. KENDRY.
(Peterborough West.)

James Kendry was born in Oshawa, Ont., on March 29, 1845. English descent. His father came to Canada in 1841 from Yorkshire, England, and his mother came to Canada about the same time from Paisley, Scotland. His father has been engaged in the woolen business all his lifetime. The subject of this sketch followed up the same business. After leaving the Public School where he received his education he entered the service of Barber Bros., at Streetsville, Ont., where he remained some time. He afterwards became manager of the Clyde Woolen Mills at Lanark, Ont., for Boyd Caldwell; was also manager and interested in the firm of Glen Tay, with Moorehouse, Dodds & Co, leaving there to accept the managership of the Auburn Woolen Co. of Peterboro, and is at present President and Managing Director and one of the principal owners of that Company, where he has been for the last 18 years. He is also interested in a number of manufacturing enterprises in Peterboro. Mr. Kendry has been a Councillor for 9 years, was Mayor of Peterboro for 4 years, and has been a member of the Board of Education for a number of years. He was always actively engaged in politics, and was first returned to Parliament at the general elections of 1896. A Conservative.—*Peterborough, O.*

R. M. S MIGNAULT, M.D.
(Yamaska.)

Roch Moise Samuel Mignault was born in Montreal, February 5, 1837. His ancestors emigrated from Chatillon, La Seine Department, France. He was educated at L'Assomption College. Mr. Mignault is by profession a practising physician. He is unmarried. He has held several public offices, such as Mayor and Councillor of his Municipality and J. P. He was first elected to the House of Commons at the general election held in 1891, and was re-elected at the general election of 1896. A Liberal. —*St. Michel de Yamaska, Q.*

LOUIS LAVERGNE.
(Drummond and Arthabaska.)

Louis Lavergne was born at St. Pierre, County of Montmagny, December 1, 1845, his father being the late David Lavergne, Esq., of St. Pierre, whose ancestors came from Limoges, France, in 1650, his mother being Marie Genevieve Delagrave, whose ancestors came from Berri, France, in 1750. He was educated at St. Anne's College, County of Kamouraska. He is by profession a notary, and is also Editor of *L'Unions des Cantons de l'Est*. He was married first, in 1878, to Eugenie, daughter of Dr. L. E. Landry, of Bécancour, who died in 1887; second, to Alida Pacaud, widow of the late William Duval. He is Sec.-Treas. of the Agricultural Society of the County of Arthabaska, Secretary-Treasurer and Clerk of the same County, Secretary-Treasurer of the Board of School Commissioners of Arthabaskaville and St. Christophe, and Church Warden of the Parish of St. Christophe d'Arthabaska. He was first returned to Parliament November 13, 1897, at the by-election necessitated by the elevation of his brother to the Bench by a majority of 1,648 over the Conservative candidate. A Liberal.—*Arthabaskaville, Q.*

WILLIAM McCLEARY.
(Welland.)

William McCleary was born in Thorold, November 5, 1853. His father and mother were both natives of the County of Monaghan, Ireland, who emigrated to Canada in 1842, and settled in Thorold. He was educated at the Public and Grammar Schools, and also in Toronto. He is engaged in business as a lumber merchant. Has been Warden of the County of Welland and also Councillor, Reeve and Mayor of Thorold. He married in December, 1877, Jennie, daughter of the late J. T. Ewart, Esq. In 1890 he was appointed to the Legislative Assembly of Ontario, and sat there until 1894. He was first elected to the House of Commons at the general elections of 1896. A Conservative.—*Thorold, O.*

W. J. LEWIS, M.D.
(Albert.)

William James Lewis was born at Hillsborough, September 25, 1830, and is the son of the late Hon. John Lewis, M.L.C., New Brunswick. He was educated at Hillsborough and at the Sackville Academy. He is a Doctor of Medicine of the University of Glasgow and also a member of the College of Surgeons, Edinburgh, Scotand. Mr. Lewis married first, in 1877, Melissa, daughter of Richard E. Steeves, Esq., of Hillsborough, and second, in 1885, Catherine, daughter of Mr. John Duffy. He held a seat in the Executive Council of New Brunswick from July 5, 1882, until February, 1883. At the general elections of 1878, he was first electted to the House of Assembly of New Brunswick, and occupied a seat in that body until his resignation in June, 1896, to run for the Commons, when he was elected to his present seat. An Independent.—*Hillsborough, N.B.*

E. G. PENNY.
(St. Lawrence Division, Montreal.)

Edward Goff Penny was born in the City of Montreal in the year 1858, and is the son of the late Hon. Senator Edward Goff Penny, the well-known journalist, for a long period editor and proprietor of the Montreal *Herald*. He was educated in Montreal, and married a daughter of Mr. J. W. Gilmour, a merchant there. Mr. Penny first came into public notice when he contested St. Lawrence Ward for the position of Alderman in 1894, an office which he has filled since then with great acceptance to his constituents. At the general elections of 1896 he was nominated in the Liberal interests against Mayor Wilson-Smith, who stood as an Independent Liberal-Conservative, and after an exciting contest was returned by a very considerable majority over Mr. Smith, whose career as Mayor up to that time had given so much satisfaction that he was considered a remarkably strong candidate. A Liberal.—*Montreal.*

D'ALTON McCARTHY, Q.C.
(North Simcoe.)

D'Alton McCarthy, Q.C., was born at Oakley Park, near Dublin, October 10, 1836, his father being a solicitor of that city. He was educated at Rev. Mr. Harnman's School, Blackrock; at Rev. Mr. Flynn's School, Dublin, and at Barrie Grammar School. He was called to the Bar of Upper Canada, Hilary term, 1858, and appointed a Q.C. December 18, 1872. He is a Bencher of the Law Society of Ontario. Mr. McCarthy is a prominent figure in Canadian politics, and was President for many years of the Liberal-Conservative Association of North Riding of Simcoe. He contested North Simcoe unsuccessfully in 1872 and twice in 1874. Was first returned to Parliament for Cardwell, December 14, 1876, and successfully contested his present seat at the general elections of 1878, to which he has been re-elected at the general elections of 1882, 1887 and 1891. At the general elections of 1896 he was returned for both North Simcoe and Brandon, but elected to sit for his old constituency. Mr. McCarthy was for some years President of the Agricultural Society of the West Riding of Simcoe. He has been twice married. A Liberal-Conservative.—*Toronto, Ont.*

GEORGE McCORMICK.
(Muskoka and Parry Sound.)

George McCormick was born in the County of Ottawa, Province of Quebec, October 7, 1856. He carries on an extensive trade in the lumber business. Elected to the Town Council, Orillia, by acclamation, and served on the board for the year 1894, but refused acclamation in 1895 to the same position. He first entered politics as a candidate for Parry Sound in the Legislative Assembly of Ontario at the general elections of 1890, but was unsuccessful. At the general elections of 1896 he contested the seat for the Commons, and was successful. A Liberal-Conservative.—*Orillia, O.*

HON. G. E. FOSTER, B.A., D.C.L., LL.D.
(York, N.B.)

Hon. George Eulas Foster was born in Carleton County, N. B., September 3, 1847, and is descended from a U. E. Loyalist, who settled in that Province in 1783. He was educated at the Common and Superior Schools in King's County, and at the University of New Brunswick, where he graduated B. A., June, 1868. He also studied at Edinburgh, Scotland, University and at Heidelberg in Germany. He was at different periods Principal of Victoria Co. Grammar School; Sunbury Co. Superior School; Classical and Mathematical teacher Baptist Academy, Fredericton; and Principal of the Ladies' High School, Fredericton; Professor of Classics and History in the University of New Brunswick. He received the degree of D.C.L. from Acadia College, N.S., 1883, and of LL.D. from the University of New Brunswick in 1895. He was first returned to Parliament for King's in 1882, re-elected on appointment to office, and again at the general elections of 1887 and 1891. Elected for his present seat at general elections of 1896. Sworn of the Privy Council and appointed Minister of Marine and Fisheries, December 10, 1885; appointed Minister of Finance, May 29, 1888, which office he held until July, 1896, when the Tupper Administration resigned. Has held the highest positions in connection with the Temperance movement in Canada and the United States. A Liberal-Conservative.—*Ottawa.*

A. F. MacLAREN.

(North Perth.)

A. F. MacLaren was born at Perth, Lanark County, Ont., his parents being also natives of same place, and his grandparents being from Perthshire, Scotland. He removed with his parents when a mere child to the county of Perth, Cromarty village, Tp. Hibbert and, strange to say, he now represents North Perth in the House of Commons. He is manufacturer of the famous MacLaren Imperial cheese. He went to Public School for a few years in Hibbert Tp., and began to work on a farm when about 10 years old. When about 17 years old began to learn the cheese business in Fullarton factory, then in Black Creek factory. A few years later, began buying cheese for the Hon. Thomas Ballantyne, then for the Ingersoll Packing Co. He was judge of cheese at World's Fair in company with Geo. E. Perlee, of New York, and A. H. Barber, of Chicago. Farming speaks of Mr. McLaren as being one of the most able and energetic executive officers of The Butter and Cheese Association of Western Ontario. He was on the Board for many years, and is now President of that Association. Has been President of the Young Liberal-Conservative Association of Stratford. Was first elected to Parliament June 23, 1896. A Conservative.—*Stratford, O.*

C. H. PARMALEE.

(Shefford.)

Charles Henry Parmalee was born at Waterloo, Province of Quebec, June 1, 1855. He was educated at the same place. Mr. Parmelee is the editor and proprietor of the *Waterloo Advertiser*. He has been Secretary-Treasurer of Waterloo and a Member of the Municipal Council. He married in 1887, Christina, daughter of Henry Rose, Esq., of Waterloo. In 1893 he was appointed President of the Eastern Townships Press Association. He was first elected to the House of Commons at the general elections held in 1896. A Liberal.—*Waterloo, Q.*

G. R. MAXWELL.

(Burrard.)

George Ritchie Maxwell was born in Stonehouse, South Lanarkshire, Scotland, on January 11, 1857, and received his elementary education at the Subscription School there. He was put to learn the trade of weaving at the early age of eight years, but, being of a studious disposition, he, by attending evening classes and exercising the greatest economy in living, was enabled to enter the University of Glasgow at the age of 19. While there he distinguished himself in Philosophy and the cognate branches of Logic, Metaphysics, Rhetoric, Psychology, gaining the Hyndford Bursary for the same, also Latin and Greek. At the close of his University course he came to Canada, and was at once called to Sylvester, Lower Leeds, afterwards removing to Three Rivers, Que., where he resided four years. Accepting a call to the First Church, Vancouver, he labored there for six years, when he resigned to contest his present constituency at the solicitation of a convention representing the Liberal Party. A Liberal.— *Vancouver, B.C.*

W. V. PETTET.

(Prince Edward.)

William Varney Pettet was born at West Lake, County of Prince Edward, Ont., May 7, 1858. He is of U. E. L. descent, being a descendant, paternally, of Daniel Pettet, who resided at Brooklyn, N.Y., and on the maternal side he is a great-grandson of Lieut. Col. Henry Young, who was the first settler in Prince Edward County, and who was born at Jamaica Plains, L.I., N.Y., March 10, 1737. He was educated at Picton Public School, the Ontario Commercial College, and at Albert College, Belleville. He was married Sept. 21, 1884, to Minnie F., daughter of the late George W. Morrison, of Aurora. He is by occupation a farmer. He has been a member of the Hallowell Township Council. Was first elected to the House of Commons in 1896. Elected as a Patron of Industry.— *West Lake, O.*

F. A. MARCOTTE, M.D.

(Champlain.)

Francois Arthur Marcotte was born on September 25, 1866, and is the son of Francois Marcotte, merchant, of Ste. Anne de la Perade. He was educated at the Seminary of Quebec, from which institution he graduated an M.D. He holds the offices of Prefet of the County of Champlain, and is Mayor of Ste. Anne de la Perade. He was first elected to the House of Commons at the general elections held in 1896, when he defeated Mr. P. Trudel, the Liberal Candidate, by a vote of 2411 to 2035. His election was immediately contested, and was annulled in December, 1896. He was again chosen candidate in March, 1897, defeating Dr. Ferdinand Trudel, the Liberal candidate, by a majority of 127. His election being contested a second time, he took a counter petition, but was maintained in his seat. A Conservative,—*Ste. Anne de la Perade, Q.*

M. McGUGAN.

(South Middlesex.)

Malcolm McGugan is one of the new Liberal members, having been elected at the general elections by a majority of 740 over his Conservative opponent, Mr. H. B. Elliott, of the City of London. Mr. McGugan is of Highland-Scotch descent, his family having come from Argyleshire, Scotland, in 1828, and settled in the Township of Caradoc, engaging in farming. He was born in Caradoc Township, County of Middlesex, July 13, 1846, and was educated at Caradoc Public School. He is engaged in farming, but in addition to that he has been much engaged in public life. He was a Member of the Council of Caradoc from 1877 to 1886 inclusive ; Reeve for eight years from 1879 to 1886 ; is a Justice of the Peace ; Warden of the County of Middlesex in 1885 ; was appointed Clerk of the Township of Caradoc in 1886, an office which he still holds ; appointed Inspector of the Middlesex House of Refuge in 1891, and holds the office still. A Liberal.—*Mount Brydges, O.*

W. McGREGOR.

(North Essex.)

William McGregor was born at Sarnia, June 24, 1836. His parents came from Scotland in 1831. He was educated at Amherstburg, Ontario. Was Warden of Essex for a period of five years, and Reeve of Windsor for six years. He married in May, 1866, Jessie L., daughter of the Rev. Robert Peden, of Hamilton, Ont. Was first elected to Parliament at the general election of 1874, but was unseated in August, 1874, and was re-elected in October, 1874. At the general elections of 1878 and 1882 he was a candidate, but was defeated. He was re-elected at the general elections of 1891 and 1896. A Liberal.—*Windsor, O.*

W. W. B. McINNES.

(Vancouver.)

William Wallace Burns McInnes, returned at the general elections as one of the four first Liberal members ever returned to the Dominion Parliament from British Columbia, is the youngest son of Senator Thomas R. McInnes, of British Columbia, and was born in Dresden, Ont., April 8, 1871. He was educated at the High School, New Westminster, B. C., and Toronto University, where he graduated B.A. in 1889. He studied law at Osgoode Hall, Toronto, and was admitted to the Bar in British Colnmbia in 1893. Mr. McInnes is a young man of brilliant powers, being a ready speaker, a keen and fearless debater, and fas great capacity for mastering all the points of his subject and placing hem lucidly and forcibly before his audience, He is the youngest member in the present Parliament by several years, and was chosen to move the address in reply to the Speech from the Throne at its opening, on which occasion he made a most effective maiden speech. He will undoubtedly do credit to the constituency which elected him, and is sure to make his mark on the floor of the House. A Liberal.—*Nanaimo, B.C.*

FIRMAN McCLURE

(Colchester.)

Firman McClure was born at Truro, N. S., November 19, 1868. He is the grandson of Alexander McClure, of Ayr, Scotland, and a son of John McClure and Susan Kent, of Truro, N.S. Was educated in Truro, and graduated at the Provincial Normal School in 1877. Married, October 28, 1896, Dora M. Inglis, of Lunenburg. He studied law with the Hon. F. A. Laurence, now Speaker of the House of Assembly of Nova Scotia, from 1878 to 1882, and was admitted to the Bar in 1882. In the same year he became a partner with Mr. Laurence, and continued so until 1888. He was editor of the *Guardian* at Truro, N.S., from 1888 to 1892, and was also editor of the *Temperance Index* from 1891 to 1892. He was Grand Worthy Patriarch of the Sons of Temperance of Nova Scotia in 1891. In June, 1896, he was a candidate for the Commons, but was defeated. He was elected to the House of Assembly at a by-election held in 1896, and served one session, and in April, 1897, he was elected for Colchester to the Commons. A Liberal.—*Truro, N.S.*

C. F. McISAAC.

(Antigonish.)

Colin Francis McIsaac was born in Antigonish in 1856. His family came from Inverness-shire, Scotland. He was appointed a Governor of St. Francis Xavier College of Antigonish in 1882. He was called to the Bar of Nova Scotia in January, 1880. In April, 1891, he was appointed a Member of the Executive Council of Nova Scotia, without portfolio. He held a seat in the House of Assembly of Nova Scotia for the County of Antigonish from the general elections held in 1886 until March, 1895, when he resigned his seat, and was elected at a federal by-election to fill the vacancy caused by the death of the late Sir J. S. D. Thompson, and was re-elected in 1896. A Liberal.—*Antigonish. N.S.*

H. F. McDOUGALL.
(Cape Breton.)

Hector Francis McDougall was born at Christmas Island, Cape Breton, N S., June 6, 1848. He is the son of Malcolm McDougall, merchant, and Mary McNeil, whose parents came from the Island of Barra, Scotland. He was educated at Christmas Island. Mr. McDougall is a merchant and farmer. On September 17, 1878, he entered the N. S. Provincial Parliament, and in October of the same year was sworn a member of the Holmes-Thompson Government of that Province. He resigned his portfolio in May, 1882, and ran for the Dominion House of Commons, but was unsuccessful. He was first elected to the House of Commons at a by-election held in 1884, and was re-elected in 1887, 1891 and 1896, representing the same constituency as Sir Charles Tupper, Bart., now represents. Mr. McDougall was principally instrumental in urging upon the Government, in 1886, the advisability of building an extension of the Intercolonial Railway through the Island of Cape Breton, which now turns out to be one of the best paying sections of that railway. A Liberal-Conservative.—*Christmas Island, C.B., N.S.*

J. McMILLAN.
(South Huron.)

John McMillan was born in Kirkconnell, Dumfrieshire, Scotland, July 19, 1823. His parents afterwards removed to Canada. He was educated in the Parish School at his native place. He has been married twice; first, on July 20 1849, to Miss Janet McMichael, and, second, to Mrs. Ann Jamieson, on November 2, 1868. He is by occupation a farmer. He was appointed a member of the Agricultural Commission of Ontario, April 3, 1880. Has been Reeve of the Township of Hallett for eleven years. Was first elected to the House of Commons for South Huron at the general elections of 1882, and resigned in 1883; re-elected at the general elections of 1887, 1891 and 1896. A Liberal.—*Constance, O.*

ALEXANDER MARTIN,

(East Queens, P.E.I.)

Alexander Martin was born in March, 1842, at Springton, P.E.I., being a son of the late Alexander Martin, a native of Uigg, in the Isle of Skye, Scotland. He was educated at the common schools, Normal School and Academy, Charlottetown, P.E.I. Mr. Martin is a farmer and merchant. He married in 1859, Anne, daughter of the late Roderick McLeod, of Uigg, P.E.I. He represented Belfast, P.E.I, in the Legislature of that Province for four years, and was afterwards elected to the Legislative Council, in which he sat until 1889, when he resigned. He was elected for the first time to the Dominion Parliament, June 23, 1896, when he defeated William Welsh, of Keppoch, who had represented the constituency in the House of Commons for two parliamentary terms, by a majority of 35. A Liberal-Conservative.—*Valleyfield, P.E.I.*

G. V. McINERNEY, A.M., LL.B., Q.C.

(Kent, N.B.)

George Valentine McInerney was born at Kingston, Kent County, N. B., February 14, 1857. He is the son of the late Hon. Owen McInerney, who came to Canada from Longford, Ireland, and in 1826 settled in Miramichi, N.B. He was educated at the common school at Kingston, St. Joseph's College, and at Laval University. He also studied at Harvard University and Boston University Law Schools, and in 1877 he received the degree of LL.B. In 1878 he was called to the Bar of New Brunswick, and appointed Q.C. in 1894. He married, in September, 1882, Christina, only daughter of Henry O'Leary, Esq. He is U. S. Consular Agent at Richibucto ; Secretary of the St. Louis, Richibucto & Buctouche Railway, and has been since 1880 Secretary of the Municipality of Kent. At a by-election held in December, 1892, he was first elected to the Commons, and was re-elected at the general elections of 1896. A Liberal-Conservative.—*Richibucto, N. B.*

J. McMULLEN.

(North Wellington.)

James McMullen is the second son of Archibald McMullen, who immigrated from County Monaghan, Ireland, in 1846, and settled near Fergus, Ont. Born in the County of Monaghan in 1833, and came with his father to Canada in 1846. Was educated at the Common School, Fergus. Married September 30, 1858, Mary Ann, youngest daughter of Robert Dunbar, Esq., late of Guelph, Ont. Was a merchant doing a general business in Mount Forest, where he still lives, for thirty years. Has been a member of the Crown Council, and was also Reeve for several years. Was a Director and Vice-President of the Georgian Bay and Wellington Railway, and a Director of the Grand Trunk, Georgian Bay and Lake Erie Railway, and is a Director of the Dominion Life Insurance Company. First returned to Parliament at general elections in 1882, again in 1887, 1891 and 1896. He is in favor of the policy and principles of the Reform Party as adopted at the Dominion Liberal Convention, held in Ottawa, 20th June, 1893. A Liberal.—*Mount Forest, O.*

ALEXANDER McNEILL.

(North Bruce.)

Alexander McNeill was born at The Corran, County of Antrim, Ireland, May 10, 1842. He is the son of the late Malcolm McNeill, Esq., of The Corran. His mother was a sister of the late Lord Colonsay, Lord President of the Court of Session, Scotland, and of the Right Hon. Sir John McNeill, G.C.B. He was educated at Wimbledon, Surrey, England, and at Trinity College, Dublin. He married in 1872 Hester Law Howard, daughter of the late Forbes McNeill, Esq., of Winkfield, Berks, England. Mr. McNeill is by profession a Barrister of the Middle Temple, London, Eng., and is also interested in farming. Was first elected to the House of Commons at the general elections of 1882, and was re-elected at those of 1887, 1891 and 1896. A Liberal-Conservative.—*Wiarton, Ont.*

HON. W. H. MONTAGUE.

(Haldimand.)

Walter Humphries Montague was born at Adelaide, Ont., November 21, 1858, being the son of Joseph I. and Rhoda Montague, and of English descent. Dr. Montague was educated at the Common School, High School, Woodstock College, Victoria University and Toronto School of Medicine. He is a Licentiate of the Royal College of Physicians and Surgeons, Edinburgh, and a member of the College of Physicians and Surgeons of Ontario. He contested the representation of Monk in the Legislative Assembly of Ontario, but was defeated. He entered the Dominion Parliament at the general elections in 1887, and, afterwards being unseated, was re-elected at a by-election held in November, 1887, but was again unseated and at a by-election held June, 1889, was defeated ; this election was also annulled, and in a by-election of February, 1890, Dr. Montague was once more elected, and was re-elected at the general elections held in 1891 and 1896. He entered Sir Mackenzie Bowell's Government without portfolio in 1894. Became Secretary of State, March 25, 1895, and Minister of Agriculture, January 15, 1896, retiring on the resignation of Sir Charles Tupper, Bart., on July 8, 1896. A Conservative.—*Dunnville, O.*

D. B. MEIGS.

(Missisquoi.)

Daniel Bishop Meigs was born in Henryville, County of Iberville, Que., June 1, 1835. His father and mother were both natives of Swanton, Vt., but in 1832 removed into Canada. He was educated at Bedford. He married, first, in 1866, Margaret L. Allsop, and second, in 1872, Margaret Rosa Faulkner. Mr. Meigs is by occupation a farmer. He was Mayor of Farnham several years. Was first elected to the House of Commons in 1887, and occupied the seat vacated through the death of Mr. Clayes, the sitting member. Was re-elected in 1896. A Liberal. *Farnham, Q.*

A. McLENNAN, M.D.

(Inverness.)

Angus McLennan was born at Broad Cove, Inverness County, in 1844. His paternal ancestors were natives of Kintail, Scotland. He was educated at the Grammar School at Broad Cove, at the St. Francis Xavier College, Antigonish, at Harvard University, and at the University of Penna, Philadelphia, where he graduated an M.D. in 1872. He held a seat in the House of Assembly of Nova Scotia from January, 1883, until June, 1886. Mr. McLennan was a member of the Municipal Council of Inverness to June, 1896. He was first elected to the House of Commons at the general elections held in 1896. A Liberal.—*Margaree, C.B., N.S.*

J. B. MORIN.

(Dorchester.)

Jean Baptiste Morin was elected for Parliament for the first time at the last election. He was born at Ste. Henedine, County Dorchester, Que., on September 22, 1840. He is descended from an old French family which emigrated to Canada about the year 1840. Mr. Morin traces his lineage in Canada from that stock back as far as 1741. He was educated at Ste. Henedine School, and has been for many years engaged in the lumber and coal business in Pennsylvania, U. S., in which he has been very successful. He was elected Mayor of Ste. Henedine in 1889, and still holds that office. He was chosen Warden of Dorchester County in 1892, and was made Justice of the Peace the same year. In 1893 he was elected President of the School Board, and at the general elections was chosen to represent Dorchester County in the Dominion Parliament by a majority of 330. Mr. Morin is a shrewd business man, with a thorough knowledge of business affairs, and will be a valuable member of the House. The interests of his constituents as well as those of the County at large will be carefully guarded and served by him. A Conservative.—*Ste. Henedine, Dorchester, Q.*

T. O. DAVIS.

(Saskatchewan.)

Thomas Osborne Davis was born in Sherrington, Que., in August, 1856. He is a nephew as well as namesake of Thos. Osborne Davis, the Irish poet and journalist, the author of Fontenoy. Mr. Davis' father, Samuel Davis, emigrated from Ireland in 1830, and settled in Quebec Province. He was a teacher by profession, and was Principal of the High School in Rouse's Point for several years. He educated his own family, the subject of this sketch amongst the number. About 18 years ago young Davis left his father's home to push his fortunes in the then comparatively new west. He had no money, but plenty of that pluck and energy that characterizes the Irish race. He went to work at anything his hands found to do, and pushed himself forward until he became one of the most prosperous business men and ranchers in the locality in which he settled. He has twice been elected Mayor of the thriving town of Prince Albert, Chairman of the Board of Trade, Chairman of the Public School Board; he has also held a Commission of the Peace for the Territories for several years. In 1885 he married Rebecca Jennings, a daughter of Richard Jennings, Esq., of Dublin, Ireland. First returned to Parliament at by-election held December, 1896. A Liberal.—*Prince Albert, N.W.T.*

E. B. OSLER.

(West Toronto.)

Edmund Boyd Osler was born at Tecumseh, County of Simcoe, in 1845. He is the fourth son of the late Rev. F. L. Osler, M.A. (Cantab.), formerly of Falmouth, England, and Rector of Dundas and Ancaster, and Ellen Free Pickton. Mr. Osler was President of the Board of Trade, Toronto, 1896, and is a Director of the Canadian Pacific Railway and of the Dominion Bank. He is by occupation a share broker. He was first elected to the House of Commons at the general elections held in 1896. A Conservative.—*Toronto, O.*

R. H. POPE.

(Compton.)

Rufus Henry Pope was born at Cookshire, September 13, 1857, and is the son of the late Hon. John Henry Pope, M.P., who was Minister of Railways at the time of his death in April, 1889. He was educated at the Cookshire Academy, and at Sherbrooke High School and McGill College Law School. Mr. Pope is extensively engaged in farming, and is also a breeder of thoroughbred cattle. He married Lucy, daughter of Major C. Noble, of Compton. He was first elected to the House of Commons in May, 1889, to fill the vacancy caused by the death of his father. He was re-elected at the general elections held in 1891 and 1896. A Liberal-Conservative.—*Cookshire, Q.*

W. J. POUPORE.

(Pontiac.)

William Joseph Poupore was born on Allumette Island, Que., April 29, 1846, and is of Norman-French descent. He was educated on the Island and at Ottawa College, and afterwards studied Law for two years. Carries on a large business as mill owner, contractor, and lumberer, and owns a considerable area of timber limits on the Upper Ottawa, and elsewhere. Is President of the Grand Calumet Mining Co., of Ottawa, Ltd. He constructed the Aylmer Water Works in 1895, and is a half owner of that property with his partner, J. B. Fraser, Esq., of Ottawa. He was married in 1870 to Eleonore, second daughter of the late John Poupore, Esq., formerly M.P. for Pontiac. He was Mayor of Chichester for ten years 1872-1882, and Warden of the County Pontiac in 1881-1882, when he resigned on his being elected to the Quebec Legislature in that year, which seat he held till the general elections of 1892. He was Chairman of the School Commissioners of Chichester from 1872 to 1882 inclusive. First returned to the Commons at the last general elections in 1896. An Independent-Conservative.—*Morrisburg, O.*

AULAY MORRISON, LL.B.

(New Westminster.)

Aulay MacAulay Morrison was born at Baddeck, County of Victoria, Nova Scotia, June 15, 1863, and is a son of the late Christopher Morrison. His grandfather on the maternal side, Aulay MacAulay, came from Harris, Scotland, and settled in Cape Breton. Mr. Morrison was educated in the Common Schools, at the Academies of Sydney and Pictou and at Dalhousie University, Halifax, from which he graduated with the degree of Bachelor of Law in 1888. In the same year he was called to the Bar of Nova Scotia, and to that of British Columbia in 1890, to which Province he had removed for the practice of his profession. He is a Commissioner of the New Westminster Public Library, and is also a member of the Board of Trade. He was first returned to Parliament at the general elections of 1896. A Liberal.—*New Westminster, B.C.*

H. A. POWELL.

(Westmoreland.)

Henry A. Powell was born at Richibucto, N.B., April 6, 1855, and is descended from an old Loyalist family who settled near Gagetown on the St. John River at the close of the Revolutionary War. He was educated at Kent County Grammar School, and at Mount Allison University, from which he graduated in 1875. He was called to the Bar of New Brunswick in 1880, and appointed Queen's Counsel in 1894. He was returned to the House of Assembly at the general elections of 1890, but the election was protested, and he resigned; was re-elected, and again, in 1891, after being unseated. He was re-elected in 1892, and sat in the House of Assembly until August, 1895, when he resigned to contest his present seat for the Commons. He was successful, and again at the general elections of 1896. Mr. Powell is a member of the Board of Governors of Mount Allison University. He was married on June 26, 1878, to Allie, daughter of the Rev. G. B. Payson.—*Sackville, N.B.*

F. D. MONK.

(Jacques Cartier.)

Frederick Debartzch Monk was born in Montreal, April 6, 1856, being the fourth son of the late Hon. Mr. Justice Monk, whose family came originally from Devonshire, England. His mother was Rosalie Caroline Debartzch, who came from a French family established in Canada under the French rigime. Mr. Monk was educated at the Montreal Seminary, and is by profession an advocate. He was appointed a Q.C. in 1893. He is a professor of Constitutional Law in Laval University, and was for twelve years a member of the Montreal School Board. He married, in 1880, Marie Louise, daughter of D. H. Senecal, advocate, and granddaughter of the late C. S. Cherrier, Q.C. He was first returned to Parliament, June 23, 1896, when he defeated his opponent, Mr. Arthur Boyer, by a vote of 2,329 against 2,216. A Conservative.—*Montreal.*

R. F. PREFONTAINE.

(Maisonneuve.)

Raymond Fournier Prefontaine was born in Longueuil, Que., on September 16, 1850. He was educated at the Jesuits' College, Montreal, and by private tuition. On June 20, 1876, he married Hermantine, daughter of the late Senator J. B. Rolland, of Montreal. He received the degree of B.C.L. from McGill University, and was called to the Bar of Lower Canada in 1873. From 1878 to 1884, he was Mayor of Hochelaga, and he is now Mayor of Montreal, and was for ten years the Chairman of the Board of Works, of Montreal. He is the President of the Young Liberals Association of Canada. He held a seat in the Quebec Assembly from the general elections of 1875 until the general elections held in 1878, when he was defeated. Upon the successful candidate being unseated, he was re-elected June 26, 1879, and sat until he was again defeated. He was elected for Chambly in July, 1886, and re-elected at the general elections of 1887, 1891 and 1896. A Liberal.—*Montreal.*

LIEUT.-COL. HON. E. G. PRIOR, P.C.

(Victoria City.)

Lieut.-Col. Hon. Edward Gawler Prior was born at Dallowgill, Yorkshire, England, May 21, 1853, and is the second son of the Rev. Henry Prior. He was educated at Leeds Grammar School and served his articles at Wakefield, as a Mining Engineer. He married in January, 1878, Suzette, youngest daughter of the late John Work, Esq., of Hillside, Victoria, since deceased. Col. Prior was for two years President of the Dominion Artillery Association, and is Vice-President of the Dominion Rifle Association, and commands the 5th Regt. Can. Artillery. He is by occupation a hardware merchant. In 1889 he was appointed Honorary A. D. C. to the Governor-General of Canada, and in 1890 was Commandant of the Canadian Rifle Team at Bisley. He held a seat in the Legislative Assembly of British Columbia from July, 1886, until January, 1888. He was first elected to Parliament in January, 1888, and was re-elected in 1890 and in January, 1896, and was sworn of the Privy Council, and appointed Comptroller of Inland Revenue in the Bowell Government. He resigned from the Cabinet in July, 1896. A Conservative.—*Victoria, B.C.*

C. I. RINFRET, M.D.

(Lothinière.)

Côme Isaie Rinfret, M.D., was born September 6, 1847, at Cap Santé, County of Portneuf, and is a son of F. J. Rinfret, Esq., merchant, his mother being a sister of the Hon. Isidore Thibaudeau. He was educated at the Seminary of Quebec, and studied medicine at Victoria University, Montreal, from which he graduated with the degree of M.D. He was married to Miss N. Laliberté in 1873 at St. Croix. He was first returned to Parliament at the general elections of 1878, and has sat continuously for his present seat since that time, having been re-elected at the general elections of 1882, 1887, 1891 and 1896.—*St. Croix, Q.*

J. B. MILLS, M.A., Q.C.
(Annapolis.)

John Burpee Mills was born at Granville Ferry, July 24, 1850, and is the youngest son of the late John Mills, Esq., of Granville Ferry. He was educated at Acadia College, Wolfville, N.S., and graduated a B.A. in 1871 and M.A. in 1877. He also attended Harvard University Law School, and was called to the Bar of Nova Scotia in 1875, and appointed Q.C. June 25, 1890. He married, first, in October, 1878, Bessie B. Corbitt, and, second, in July, 1896, Miss Agnes K. Rose. Mr. Mills is a director and holds offices in several local establishments, and was a member from 1882 until 1887 of the Municipal Council of Annapolis. Was first elected to the House of Commons at the general elections of 1887, and was re-elected in 1891 and 1896. A Liberal-Conservative—*Annapolis N.S.*

R. L. RICHARDSON.
(Lisgar.)

Robert Lorne Richardson was born in the County Lanark, Ont., June 28, 1860, of Scotch and English parentage, his grandfather, on his mother's side, being a Trafalgar Veteran, who settled in the County of Lanark about 80 years ago. Mr. Richardson was educated at the Balderson Public School, and became a journalist at 19 years of age, when he entered the staff of the Montreal *Star*, afterwards being attached to the *Toronto Globe*. He went to Winnipeg in 1882, where he has since resided, being all that period engaged in active daily newspaper work. In 1889, in conjunction with an old schoolmate and friend, he established the *Winnipeg Daily Tribune*, of which he is still the editor. He entered Parliament at the general elections of 1896, when he was elected member for Lisgar, defeating the Conservative candidate, Mr. R. Rodgers, by a vote of 2,687 against 2,603. He married March 11, 1885, Clara, daughter of the late Ira Mallory, of Mallorytown. A Liberal.—*Winnipeg, Man.*

DOMINIQUE MONET.

(Laprairie and Napierville.)

Dominique Monet was born at St. Michel de Napierville, January 2, 1865, and is the son of Dominique Monet, a farmer of the same place. He was educated at L'Assomption College and at Laval University, from which institution he graduated an LL.D. In July, 1889, he was called to the Bar of the Province of Quebec, and now practices in partnership with Mr. J. A. Geoffrion. He married in June, 1887, Marie Louise LaHaye. He was the Liberal candidate at the by-election of Napierville, Dec. 9, 1890, and was defeated by Mr. Paradis, Conservative. He was first elected to the House of Commons at the general elections of 1891 for the same County of Napierville by a majority of 18, and was re-elected at the general elections of 1896 in the united County of Laprairie and Napierville, by a majority of 276, against L. C. Pelletier, the previous representative of Laprairie. A Liberal-Intransigeant.—*St.Rémi of Napierville, Q.*

JAMES ROBINSON.

(Northumberland, N.B.)

James Robinson was born at Derby, N.B., being of Scotch descent, his parents having come from Scotland. He was educated at Derby, N.B. He married in 1877, Miss Grace McDonald. Mr. Robinson is a merchant and lumberman, and is manager of the South-West Miramichi Boom & Lumber Co., and is also a director of the Newcastle Miramichi Spool Factory, Ltd. He has been a County Councillor since the year 1879, and was Warden of the County for three years. He sat in the House of Assembly of New Brunswick from January, 1890, until January, 1896, when he resigned, but was afterwards elected for his present seat in the House of Commons at a by-election held to fill the vacancy caused by the appointment of the sitting member to the Senate. He was re-elected at the general elections held in 1896. A Conservative.—*Millerton, N.B.*

LIEUT.-COL. R. R. McLENNAN.

(Glengarry.)

Lt.-Col. Roderick R. McLennan was born at Glen Donald, Charlottenburg, in January, 1842. Educated there. Unmarried. Third son of Roderick McLennan, Esq., of Charlottenburg, Glengarry, and grandson of Farquhar McLennan, of Kintail, Ross-shire, Scotland, who settled in Glengarry in 1802, and served throughout the war of 1812-1814 in 2nd Regiment Glengarry Militia, being present at the capture of Ogdensburg and other important engagements. Col. McLennan in his younger days was very fond of all kinds of athletic sports, and was the best all-round athlete that Canada ever produced. Was for many years engaged in construction of railways and other public works, including the most difficult section of the C.P.R. north of Lake Superior. Is a Director of the Manufacturers' Life Ins. Co., was President of the Liberal-Conservative Association for Glengarry, from 1885 to 1890. Is Colonel 59th Batt. Stormont and Glengarry Regiment. Has been active in pressing the claims of the veterans of 1837-8, for recognition and compensation. Author of an Act passed in the Session of 1896 for the protection of laborers employed by the Government and companies in the construction of public works, and has actively advocated many other measures in the interest of the working and agricultural classes. First returned to Parliament at g. e., 1891. Unseated and re-elected 14th Jan., 1892. Re-elected 1896. A Conservative.—*Alexandria, O.*

J. D. REID, M.D.

(South Grenville.)

John Dowsley Reid, M.D., was born at Prescott, Ont., January 1, 1859, his father being the late John Reid, a native of Belfast, Ireland, who came to Canada in 1845, and married a daughter of the late John Dowsley, of Prescott. Mr. Reid was educated at Queen's College, Kingston, and graduated from thence with the degree of M.D. He is unmarried. He was first returned to Parliament at the general elections of 1891, and was re-elected at the last general elections of 1896. A Conservative.—*Cardinal, O.*

HON. A. A. C. LARIVIERE.

(Provencher.)

Hon. Alphonse Alfred Clement LaRivière, third son of the late Abraham C. LaRivière, of Montreal, and Adelaide Marcil, of Longueuil, was born in Montreal, July 24, 1842, and was educated at St. Mary's College, Montreal. He was elected President of the Board of Arts and Manufactures for the Province of Quebec, the Institut des Artisans Canadiens, and the Cercle St. Pierre of Montreal, President of the Selkirk County Agricultural Society, Superintendent of the Catholic Schools, Joint Secretary of the Board of Education, and a member of the Council of the University of Manitoba. He represented St. Anne in the Manitoba Legislative Assembly in 1874. In 1878 he was elected by acclamation for St. Boniface, and again in 1879. Being appointed Provincial Secretary in 1881, he was re-elected by acclamation. In 1883 he was made Minister of Agriculture, Statistics and Health, which office he resigned in 1866 to take the Provincial Treasurership. In 1889 he was elected to represent Provencher in the Dominion House to succeed the Hon. Joseph Royal, and has been twice re-elected. A Liberal-Conservative.—*St. Boniface, Man.*

ANDREW SEMPLE.

(Centre Wellington.)

Andrew Semple was born in Glasgow, June 10, 1837. His parents were both natives of Lanarkshire, Scotland, and emigrated to Canada from Glasgow in 1841. He was educated at the Common Schools in the County of Simcoe. He was married October 19, 1866, to Margaret Potter. He is in business as a farmer and miller. He held the offices of Councillor and Reeve of East Garafraxa for two years. He is a J.P., and is also a prominent member of the I.O.F. and the A.O.U.W. He was first elected to the House of Commons at the general elections of 1887, and was re-elected at the general elections of 1891 and 1896. A Liberal.—*Fergus, O.*

JOHN R. ROBERTSON.

(East Toronto.)

John Ross Robertson was born in Toronto on December 28, 1841, his father being the late John Robertson, wholesale dry goods merchant, who came from Nairnshire, Scotland, and was directly descended from Duncan Robertson, Chief of the Clan of Struan Robertson in 1347. Mr. Robertson was educated at Upper Canada College, and has been twice married, his present wife being a daughter of George B. Holland, Esq., of Toronto. Mr. Robertson is a well-known publisher, and has been President of the Canadian Copyright Association from 1888. He is also a prominent Free Mason and was Grand-Master of the Grand Lodge of Canada in Ontario, 1890-1892; Grand First Principal of the Royal Arch Chapter of Canada in 1894-1897; also Representative of the United Grand Lodge of England in Ontario. He was first returned to Parliament at the general elections of 1896. An Independent-Liberal-Conservative.—*Toronto.*

J. A. ROSS, M.D.

(Rimouski.)

Jean Auguste Ross was born in Rimouski on September 6, 1851, his father being John Ross, which is suggestive of Scotch descent, and his mother, Caroline Talbot. He was one of two children, and was educated at Ste. Anne and Rimouski Seminaries, afterwards taking a medical course at Laval University, Quebec, from which he graduated, and soon after established himself as physician and surgeon in his native place, where at present he enjoys a wide practice. He is Coroner for the District of Rimouski, and also Quarantine Officer for that port, in which capacity he has obtained a favorable reputation among passengers by the St. Lawrence route. Dr. Ross was first elected to the Parliament of Canada at a by-election held in 1897, on the appointment of J. B. R. Fiset, M.D., to the Senate of Canada. A Liberal.—*Rimouski, Q.*

W. J. ROCHE, M.D.

(Marquette.)

William James Roche was born at Clandeboye, Ont., on November 30, 1859, his father being a native of Wexford, Ireland. He was educated at the Public School of Lucan, Ont., and at the London High School. He also attended Trinity University at Toronto, and subsequently graduated at the Western University in London, in 1883. He married July 17, 1884, Annie E., daughter of the late William Cook, of Toronto. Mr. Roche is by profession a practicing physician, and has been a member of the Manitoba Medical Council since 1884. He was Grand-Master of the Independent Order of Odd Fellows for the Province of Manitoba in 1892 and 1893, and was also Grand Representative to Sovereign Grand Lodge, which met in Chattanooga, Tenn., in 1894, and in Atlantic City, N.J., in 1895. He was an unsuccessful candidate for the Legislative Assembly in 1892. He was first returned to Parliament at the general elections of 1896. A Conservative.—*Minnedosa, Man.*

BENNETT ROSAMOND.

(North Lanark.)

Bennett Rosamond was born at Carleton Place, Ont., May 10, 1833. He is the eldest son of the late Mr. James Rosamond, who in 1827 removed to Canada from the County of Leitrim, Ireland, and of Margaret Wilson, who came from the vicinity of Paisley, Scotland. He was educated at the Grammar School in Carleton Place. Mr. Rosamond has held the offices of Chairman of the United School Board, Reeve and Mayor of Almonte. He is President and Managing Director of the Rosamond Woollen Co., and Vice-President and Managing Director of the Almonte Knitting Co. He was first elected to the Commons at a by-election held in December, 1891, to fill the seat vacated through the appointment of Mr. Jamieson, the sitting member, to a Judgeship. He was re-elected at the general elections of 1896. A Liberal-Conservative.—*Almonte, O.*

FRANK OLIVER.

(Alberta.)

Frank Oliver was born in the Township of Chinguacousy, County of Peel, Ont., September, 1853, and was educated at the Common School there. He is of mixed Irish and English descent. A journalist by profession; he is proprietor of the Edmonton *Bulletin*. Married, in 1881, Harriet, daughter of Thomas Dunlap, Prairie Grove, Man. Mr. Oliver sat for the District of Edmonton in the North-West Council from May 29, 1883, to 1884, and in the Legislative Assembly of the North-West Territories from the general elections of 1888 to June, 1896, when he resigned. At the general elections of 1896 he was elected for his present constituency to the Parliament of Canada. An Independent-Liberal.—*Edmonton, Alberta.*

J. G. SNETSINGER.

(Cornwall and Stormont.)

John Goodall Snetsinger was born in in 1833 in the Township of Cornwall. His parents were U.E. Loyalists, and his ancestors, who were of German origin, settled in Stormont about the end of the 18th century. Mr. Snetsinger was educated at Cornwall Grammar School, and started business life as a clerk in the store of the late Colonel VanKoughnet in Cornwall, shortly afterwards joining the business of A. J. Barnhart, of Barnhart's Island. About 40 years ago he established a general store and flour mills at Moulinette, Ont., which business he still carries on. He has held the office of Reeve of his own township for several years, and has been Warden of Cornwall and Stormont. He succeeded the late John Sandfield Macdonald as member for Cornwall and Stormont in the Ontario Legislature from 1871 to 1879. He contested Cornwall and Stormont unsuccessfully in 1891, reducing Dr. Bergin's majority, however, very greatly. He was first returned to the House of Commons at the general elections of 1896. A Liberal.—*Cornwall, O.*

ISIDORE PROULX.

(Prescott.)

Isidore Proulx was born at St. Hermas, Province of Quebec, March 13, 1840, and received his education at the Model School there. He was married in 1861 to Philomene Lalonde, of St. Hermas, and settled in the Township of Plantagenet in 1881. He is a farmer by occupation, but has always taken a lively interest in public affairs, and was for twenty years Clerk of the Municipality of St. Hermas, and Reeve of North Plantagenet for five years. Mr. Proulx is also a Justice of the Peace. In 1874 he ran for the Legislative Assembly of Quebec, but was unsuccessful. He was first returned to Parliament at the general elections of 1891 and was re-elected at the last general elections of 1896.—*Plantagenet, O.*

M. J. F. QUINN, Q.C.

(St. Ann's Division, Montreal.)

Michael Joseph Francis Quinn, Q.C., was born in Kingston, Ont., and was educated at the Christian Brothers School and at Regiopolis College of that city. His father came to Canada from the County Tyrone, Ireland, in 1840. He was admitted to the Bar of Quebec in 1878, and received the appointment of Q.C. in 1890. He has been Crown Prosecutor and substitute of the Attorney-General of the Province of Quebec at Montreal from March, 1892 to June, 1897. At the general elections of 1887, Mr. Quinn was an unsuccessful candidate for the County of Chateauguay. He was first returned to Parliament at the general elections of 1896. Mr. Quinn has been twice married; first to Elizabeth, a daughter of the late John Harty, Esq., of Peterborough, Ont., who died in 1885; and, secondly, in 1889, to Ellen Mary, daughter of M. C. Mullarky, Esq., of Montreal. Mr. Quinn's election was somewhat noteworthy, he having defeated Hon. James McShane, who was exceedingly popular in the constituency, and who had represented it previously in the Commons and in the Legislative Assembly.—*Montreal.*

THOMAS G. RODDICK, M.D.

(St. Antoine Division, Montreal.)

Thomas G. Roddick was born July 31, 1846, at Harbor Grace, Newfoundland, and received his early education there, his father being Principal of the Government Grammar School. He subsequently attended the Model and Normal Schools, Truro, N.S.; entered the Medical Faculty of McGill University in 1864; graduated in 1868 with the highest honors, taking the Holmes Gold Medal and Final Prize. He was at once appointed Assistant House Surgeon Montreal General Hospital, and, after spending six years there in various capacities, retired in 1874 to take a position on the attending staff. In connection with the McGill Medical Faculty, he was appointed Lecturer on Hygiene, 1872; Demonstrator of Anatomy, 1874; and the following year Professor of Clinical Surgery; held the latter position for 15 years, when he was promoted to the Chair of Surgery on the retirement of the late Dr. G. E. Fenwick. He is now Consulting Surgeon to both the General and Royal Victoria Hospitals. He has served on the Militia Force as Assistant Surgeon Grand Trunk Rifle Brigade, and Surgeon Major Prince of Wales Rifles. On the outbreak of the North-West Rebellion in 1885, he was selected to take charge of medical affairs in the field, with the rank of Deputy-Surgeon General of Militia. He organized the hospitals and medical service for the Expeditionary Force, and was recommended for C.M.G. by the General in command. Was President of the Canadian Medical Association in 1891, and is now President of the British Medical Association. The doctor married, 1880, Miss McKinnon, daughter of the late Wm. McKinnon, Esq., of Willow Bank, Pointe Claire, who died in 1890. Was returned to Parliament at the general elections of 1896. A Conservative.—*Montreal.*

VALENTINE RATZ.

(North Middlesex.)

Valentine Ratz was born at St. Jacobs, County of Waterloo, November 12, 1848, and educated at Pine Hill Public School. He is a grandson of Valentine Ratz, who emigrated from Germany and settled on the site of the present town of Waterloo, Ont. His father, Jacob Ratz, was formerly an extensive lumberman in the Township of Wilmot, County of Waterloo. The subject of our sketch unites the occupation of lumberman with that of farmer. He is President of the South River Lumber Co. of Parry Sound Dist. He was married on February 13, 1873, to Miss Mary Yager, of New Hamburg. In 1879 he entered the Municipal Council of the Township of Stephen, and has successively filled the offices of Deputy Reeve and Reeve. He was also elected Warden of the County of Huron in 1886. He was first returned to Parliament at the general elections of 1896. A Liberal.—*Mount Carmel, O.*

DAVID D. ROGERS.

(Frontenac.)

David Dickson Rogers was born June 10, 1845, in County Monaghan, Ireland, leaving that country same year for Canada. His parents settled in Prince Edward County, where he remained for fifteen years, removing thirty-five years ago to County Frontenac. Mr. Rogers, who is a farmer, was educated at the Kingston Collegiate Institute. He is a Director and President of the Farmers' Institute and Agricultural Association. He practices mixed farming, and takes an active interest in everything pertaining to the agricultural class. Mr. Rogers was formerly a Conservative, but was elected as a Patron of Industry at the general elections of 1896, being the only member west of Montreal elected by acclamation. He married, in 1883, Charlotte, second daughter of the late Colin McNab. A Patron of Industry.—*Pittsburgh, O.*

BENJAMIN RUSSELL.
(Halifax.)

Benjamin Russell was born at Dartmouth, N.S., January 10, 1849. He is the son of N. Russell, and a grandson of Nathaniel Russell, who at the time of the evacuation of Boston by the British removed to Nova Scotia. He was educated at the Halifax Grammar School and at Mount Allison College. He was married September 4, 1872, to Louise, daughter of Captain Coleman, of Dartmouth. He is by profession a Barrister-at-Law, and is also Recorder of Dartmouth, and Professor of the Law of Contracts in Dalhousie University. He has also held the position of Reporter to the Supreme Court, and legal adviser of the Legislative Council of Nova Scotia. He was first elected to the House of Commons at the general election held in 1896. A Liberal.—*Halifax, N.S.*

W. STUBBS.
(Cardwell.)

William Stubbs was born July 11, 1847, in the Township of Caledon, his parents being natives of the County Fermanagh, Ireland, who came to Canada in 1824, and settled in the Township of Caledon. Mr. Stubbs is a veterinary surgeon and farmer. He was educated in the Public School, and at the Veterinary College of Medicine, Toronto, where he graduated in March, 1868. In 1888 he married Annie, daughter of the late William Gillespie, of Orangeville. Has been first Deputy Reeve and Reeve of the Township of Caledon for several years, and has been Judge at nearly all the fairs in his district. He has held the position of Ontario Government Veterinary Surgeon for the District of Peel and Cardwell. He was first returned to Parliament at the by-election held in Cardwell December 24, 1895, and was re-elected at the general election in 1896, when he defeated Mr. Walsh, the straight Conservative Candidate, by about 400 majority. Mr. Stubbs is an Independent-Conservative.—*Caledon, O.*

J. A. C. MADORE.

(Hochelaga.)

Joseph Alexandre Camille Madore was born at Blue Bonnets, Que., August 3, 1858. He was educated at the Montreal College, St. Mary's College and at McGill University, where he graduated a B.C.L. in 1880. In 1881 he was called to the Bar. He is by profession an advocate. At the general elections of 1891 he was a candidate for Jacques Cartier, but was defeated. He is a member of the General Council of the Bar for the Province of Quebec. He was first elected to the House of Commons at the general elections held in 1896. A Liberal.—*Montreal.*

T. S. SPROULE, M.D.

(East Grey.)

Dr. Thomas Simpson Sproule was born in the Township of King, York County, Ont., October 25, 1843. He is of pure Irish descent, his parents having come to Canada from County Tyrone, Ireland, in 1836, and settled in York County. Dr. Sproule received his education first in the Common Schools and the Universities of Michigan and Victoria. He graduated M.D. from the latter University in 1868, and began the practice of his profession in Kalamazoo, Mich., but soon removed to Markdale, Ont., where he has since resided, enjoying for many years a large and lucrative practice. He has also been for a long time, and still is, extensively engaged in farming and stock-raising, and for some time has been interested in the milling business. He has done good work in the promotion of agricultural societies, and was, for a time, a member of the municipality in which he resides. He was first elected to Parliament to represent East Grey in the year 1878, and again in 1882, 1887, 1891 and 1895. Was Chairman of the Committee on Agriculture and Colonization from 1892 to 1896. He is a Liberal-Conservative, a staunch advocate of Protection, and in favor of National Schools.—*Markdale, O.*

J. G. RUTHERFORD.

(Macdonald.)

John Gunion Rutherford was born at Mountain Cross, Peeblesshire, Scotland, December 25, 1857, his father being the Rev. Robert Rutherford, M.A., for nearly fifty years Minister there. He was educated at the High School, Glasgow, and by private tuition. On coming to Canada in 1875, he took a course at the Ontario Agricultural College, and afterwards attended the Ontario Veterinary College, graduating from that institution in 1879 with the rank of Gold Medalist. He is President of the Manitoba Liberal Printing Company, and also the owner of a large Veterinary Infirmary. During the North-West troubles in 1885, Mr. Rutherford served with the Winnipeg Field Battery as Veterinary Surgeon, and was present at the engagements of Fish Creek and Batoche, for which he received the medal and clasp. Married in 1887, Edith, daughter of the late Washington Boultbee, Esq., of Thornvale, Ancaster, Ont. Mr. Rutherford contested the constituency at the by-election held in May, 1897, and was successful. Has been President of the Portage and Lakeside Agricultural Society, of the Turf Club, of St. Andrew's Society, and of the Veterinary Association of Manitoba, and is now President of the Horse Breeders' Association of Manitoba and Vice-President of the Manitoba Poultry Association. He entertains a firm belief in the future of Canada as an integral portion of the British Empire. A Liberal.—*Portage la Prairie, Man.*

J. J. TUCKER.

(St. John, N.B.)

Lieutenant Colonel Joseph John Tucker was born at Chatham, Kent, England, and at an early age came to Canada with his father, the late John Tucker of St. John, N.B. Mr. Tucker was educated in England. He was for twenty years the chief surveyor for Lloyds in the East, and resided at Shanghai. He is a Lieut.-Colonel in command of the 62nd Battalion (Fusileers), St. John, N.B. Mr. Tucker was first returned to Parliament at the general elections held in 1896. A Liberal.—*St. John, N.B.*

P. V. SAVARD.

(Chicoutimi and Saguenay.)

Paul Vilmond Savard was born at Eboulements, County of Charlevoix, July 28, 1864, and received his early education at the Seminary of Chicoutimi. He also studied at Laval University, where he graduated in Law in 1886. He was married July 23, 1888, to Marie Louise, daughter of C. Dufresne, Esq., Principal of Montmagny College. He follows his profession as an advocate at the present time. Mr. Savard was an unsuccessful candidate for his present seat in the Legislative Assembly of the Province of Quebec at the general elections of 1890. He was first returned to Parliament at the general elections of 1891, but was unseated. He was re-elected at the last general elections in 1896. A Liberal.—*Chicoutimi, Q.*

HON. D. TISDALE.

(South Norfolk.)

Lieut.-Colonel the Hon. David Tisdale was born in the Township of Charlotteville, County of Norfolk, Ont., September 8, 1835. He is a grandson of Ephraim Tisdale, a U.E. Loyalist, who took part in the battles of Queenston Heights and Lundy's Lane in 1812. He was educated at the Simcoe Grammar School. He was called to the Ontario Bar in 1858, appointed a Q.C. in 1872. He joined the Militia in 1861, and commanded the 39th Norfolk Rifles V.M. from 1868 to 1876. He unsuccessfully contested North Norfolk in 1874. He was elected in South Norfolk in 1887, 1891, 1896, and on the formation of Sir Charles Tupper's Administration was appointed Minister of Militia and Defence, May 2nd, 1896. He retired of course when Sir Charles resigned. He married November 16, 1858. He was largely instrumental in constructing and financing the Grand Trunk, Georgian Bay and Lake Erie Railway Company, and has been interested in other railway construction of a successful nature. A Conservative.—*Simcoe, O.*

A. H. MOORE.

(Stanstead.)

Alvan Head Moore was born at Hatley, Stanstead County, Que., April 20, 1838. His father and mother were born in the United States, but, in 1797, joined the exodus of U. E. Loyalists, came to Canada, and settled in Stanstead County. The subject of this sketch was educated in Canadian Academies, and United States Collegiate Institutes. Was President of the Waterloo and Magog Railway at the time it was transferred to and became part of the C. P. R. Is a Director in the Stanstead, Shefford and Chambly Ry. Co. Was one of the first promoters of the Magog Print Works, and a Director in the Company until it was sold to the Dominion Cotton Mills Co. Was for a long time Mayor of the Township and Town of Magog, and Chairman of the School Commissioners, and for some time Warden of the County of Stanstead. Was for many years President of the Stanstead County Agricultural Society, a Justice of the Peace and Commissioner of the Superior Court. Married Julia A., daughter of the late Ralph Merry, Esq., of Magog. Was elected to the House of Commons at the general elections of 1896. An Independent-Conservative.—*Magog, Q.*

J. SCRIVER.

(Huntingdon.)

Julius Scriver was born at Hemmingford, P.Q., February 5, 1826. He is a descendant of U. E. Loyalists who at the close of the Revolution came to Canada from Duchess County, N.Y. He was educated at the University of Vermont. Mr. Scriver was formerly by occupation a merchant. He married Miss Frances M. Stevens, of Potsdam, N.Y. Was President of the Quebec Frontier Railway. He represented Huntingdon in the Quebec Assembly from the time of the Union until his resignation in September, 1869, and was elected by acclamation to the Commons. He was also re-elected at the general elections of 1872, 1874, 1878, 1882, 1887, 1891, 1896. A Liberal.—*Hemmingford, Q.*

JAMES SOMERVILLE.

(North Wentworth and Brant.)

James Somerville was born in Dundas, Ont., June 7, 1834. His parents emigrated to Canada from Fifeshire, Scotland, settling in Dundas in 1833. He was educated at the Common and Grammar Schools of Dundas and Simcoe. In 1854 he established the Ayr *Observer*, and was editor and proprietor until 1858, when he removed to Dundas, where he established the *True Banner*, and was editor and proprietor of that paper until 1886. He married in 1858, Janette, daughter of Mr. Alexander Rogers, Brant County, Ontario. Mr. Somerville has been Mayor of Dundas and Warden of the County of Wentworth, and has also held many municipal offices. He was first elected to the House of Commons at the general elections of 1882, and was re-elected at those of 1887, 1891 and 1896. A Liberal.—*Dundas, O.*

M. T. STENSON.

(Richmond and Wolfe.)

Michael Thomas Stenson was born December 17, 1838, at Longford, Ireland, being the son of the late John Stenson, a grain dealer of Kildare, Ireland, who came to Canada in 1840, and carried on business as a wood merchant in Montreal. Mr. Stenson was educated at St. Mary's College, Montreal, where he took a classical course, and at Ste. Anne de la Pocatière, where he took a course in agriculture; in May, 1864, obtained certificate from Military School at Montreal. He has been a farmer and a school teacher, and has held the office of Public School Inspector since 1864. He has been Mayor of Wotton and Warden of Wolfe County repeatedly, as well as director of No. 2 Wolfe County Agricultural Society, and President of Wotton Farmers' Club. He married first, in 1860, Bridget G. O'Rielly, who died 1880, and second, in 1886 Marie Rosalie Deseve, of Sherbrooke. Mr. Stenson was first returned to Parliament at the general elections of 1896. A Liberal.—*Richmond, Q.*

JAMES SUTHERLAND.

(North Oxford.)

James Sutherland was born in the Township of Ancaster, County of Wentworth, July 17, 1849. He is the son of the late Alexander Sutherland, who removed from Caithness-shire, Scotland, to Canada in 1841, and settled in the Township of Ancaster, but removed in 1855 to the Township of East Zorra, County of Oxford. He was educated at the Grammar School of Woodstock. Mr. Sutherland was for several years a Member of the Municipal Council of Woodstock, and was Mayor for the year 1880. In the same year he was appointed a member of the Collegiate Institute Board of Trustees, and has held that office ever since. He was first elected to the Commons in December, 1880, and was re-elected in 1882, 1887, 1891 and 1896, and is now Chairman of the Railway Committee of the Commons and Chief Liberal Whip. A Liberal.—*Woodstock, O.*

O. E. TALBOT.

(Bellechasse.)

Onesiphore Ernest Talbot was born at St. Arsene, County of Temiscouata, and is the son of Mr. J. F. Talbot, notary, by Marguerite, daughter of E. R. Frechette, proprietor of *Le Canadien*, who was imprisoned during the Canadian Rebellion of 1837. His ancestors came to Canada with the British Army, and after the capitulation settled in Montmagny County, moving subsequently to L'Islet County. Mr. Talbot was educated at St. Michel and at Quebec Seminary, and afterwards engaged in commercial pursuits in the United States, Ontario and Montreal until 1887, when he took to farming at St. Michel, in which latter capacity he has been very successful. Received medal and diploma, and appointed member of Agricultural Council of Province of Quebec. He was married in 1887 to Mary Guilsmartin, a Creole of Savannah, Georgia, U.S.A. He was first returned to Parliament at the general elections of 1896. A Liberal.—*St. Michel de Bellechasse, Q.*

GEORGE TAYLOR.

(South Leeds.)

George Taylor was born in the Township of Lansdowne, County of Leeds, Ont., March 31, 1840. He is the second son of the late William Taylor, Esq., and Ann Graham, who in 1818 emigrated to the County of Leeds, Ont., from the County of Wexford, Ireland. He was educated at the Common School in the Township of Lansdowne. Mr. Taylor is by occupation a merchant. He married in September, 1863, Miss Margaret Latimer. He held the offices of Warden of the United Counties of Leeds and Grenville in 1879; Reeve of Gananoque for a period of five years, and was County Auditor in 1881 and 1882. He was first elected to the Commons at the general elections of 1882, and was re-elected at those of 1887, 1891 and 1896. A Conservative.—*Gananoque, O.*

LIEUT.-COL. R. TYRWHITT.

(South Simcoe.)

Lieut.-Col. Richard Tyrwhitt was born in the County of Simcoe, Ont., November 29, 1844. He is the son of William Tyrwhitt, and grandson of Richard Tyrwhitt, Esq., of Nantyr Hall, Denbighshire. He was educated at Dinan and Rouen, France; Barrie, Ont.; and by private tuition. Mr. Tyrwhitt is Lieut.-Col. of the 36th Batt. V. M., and is engaged in farming. He married in April, 1870, Emma, daughter of the late Ven. Archdeacon G. Whitaker, Provost Trinity College, Toronto. In 1866 he was Lieut. in a provisional Batt. on the Niagara Frontier. Served in the North-West Rebellion in 1885 as senior Major, York and Simcoe Regiment (Medal). He was Commander of the Wimbledon Team in 1886. Was attached to the Canadian Contingent at Queen's Jubilee, 1897, in London (Medal). Upon the death of the sitting Member for his present seat, he was first elected to the Commons in February, 1882. He was re-elected at the general elections of 1882, 1887, 1891 and 1896. A Conservative.—*Bradford, O.*

HON. SIR CHARLES TUPPER, BART., G.C.M.G., C.B., M.D., LL.D.
(Cape Breton.)

Hon. Sir Charles Tupper, Bart., was born at Amherst, Nova Scotia, July 2, 1821, his father being the late Rev. Charles Tupper, D.D., of Aylesford, N.S. Is an M.A. and D.C.L., of Acadia College, N.S.; took the degree of M.D. at Edinburgh, and obtained the diploma of the Royal College of Surgeons in the same city in 1843. He is a Governor of Dalhousie College, Halifax; was President of the Canadian Medical Association from its formation in 1867 until 1870, when he declined re-election. To relate all the incidents in connection with Sir Charles Tupper's political career would be to write a history of Canada. There is no man at present in public life who has taken such an active part in the political affairs of this country. He entered political life as member for Cumberland in the Nova Scotia Assembly on May 22, 1855, until the Union, when he was elected to the House of Commons, in which he sat until May 24, 1884; re-elected at the general elections in 1887 and unseated for bribery by agents, but was again re-elected by an increased majority; was not a candidate at the general elections of 1891. In January, 1896, entered the Administration of Sir Mackenzie Bowell, as Secretary of State, being returned for Cape Breton; formed a Liberal-Conservative Government on the resignation of the former, in which he held the position of Prime Minister and portfolio of Secretary of State from April 27 to July 8, 1896, when he resigned consequent on the defeat of his party at the polls at the general elections held the previous month. Chosen Leader of the Opposition, August, 1896. He was a Member of the Executive Council and Provincial Secretary of Nova Scotia from 1857 to 1860, and from 1863 till June 30; Prime Minister of that Province from 1864 until he retired in 1867. Was leader of the delegation from Nova Scotia to the Union Conference at Charlottetown in 1864; to that in Quebec the same year, and to the final Colonial Conference in London to complete the terms of Confederation, 1866-67. Sworn of the Privy Council, June, 1870, he was President of that body until July, 1872, when he was appointed Minister of Inland Revenue; has also held the portfolio of Minister of Customs, Minister of Public Works, Minister of Railways and Canals, and Finance Minister. In 1884 was appointed High Commissioner for Canada in London, but re-entered the Cabinet again in 1887, and remained until May, 1888, when he again accepted the position of High Commissioner. Was one of Her Majesty's plenipotentiaries to the Fisheries' Conference at Washington in 1887. While in Parliament he has been instrumental in carrying through a large number of important measures, amongst others the Act granting a Charter to the Canadian Pacific Railway Company and the Act prohibiting the manufacture and sale of intoxicating liquors in the North-West Territories.—*Ottawa, O.*

HON. SIR CHARLES HIBBERT TUPPER, K.C.M.G.
(Pictou.)

The Hon. Sir Charles Hibbert Tupper, K.C.M.G., Q.C., was born at Amherst, N.S., August 3, 1855, and is the second son of Sir Charles Tupper, Bart. He was educated at McGill College, and at Harvard University, where he obtained the degree of LL.B. Called to the Bar of Nova Scotia in 1878, appointed Q.C. (Federal), August 2, 1890. Sworn of the Privy Council and appointed Minister of Marine and Fisheries, May 31, 1888; Minister of Justice, December 21, 1894, resigning in January, 1896. Solicitor-General (not in Cabinet) in the Administration of Sir Charles Tupper, Bart., from April 27 to July 8, 1896. Created K.C.M.G., 1893, in recognition of his services as Her Majesty's Agent in the Behring Sea Arbitration at Paris. Married, September, 1879, Janet, daughter of Hon. James McDonald, Chief Justice of Nova Scotia. First returned to Parliament in 1882; re-elected 1887, 1891, 1896, and on acceptance of office, June 18, 1888. A Liberal-Conservative.—*Victoria, B.C.*

GEORGE TURCOT.
(Megantic.)

George Turcot was born at Ste. Marie de Beauce, September 12, 1851. He was educated at the same place. Mr. Turcot has been married twice; first, in 1873, to Florida, daughter of F. X. Rousseau, who died in 1875, and, second, in 1885 to a sister of his deceased wife. After he had worked for several years on his father's farm, he started in business as a merchant. He has held the office of Chairman of the Board of School Commissioners since 1877, and also that of Secretary of the Municipal

Council of Ste. Julie for twelve years. Was unanimously elected Mayor in 1893, and Warden of the County in 1894. He has held his present seat in the House of Commons from the general elections of 1887 to the general elections of 1891, when he was an unsuccessful candidate. He was re-elected at the general elections of 1896 by defeating L. J. Frechette, Conservative, by a vote of 2073 to 1410. A Liberal.—*Ste. Julie de Somerset, Q.*

J. TOLMIE.

(West Bruce.)

John Tolmie was born in the Parish of Laggan, Inverness-shire, Scotland, August 31, 1845. He was educated at the Public School at Balgown. He was married in 1883 to Maggie H. Paterson, of Lucknow, Ont. He and his parents emigrated to Canada in 1868, and settled in Bruce Township on a farm which is still owned by him. In 1884 he removed to Kincardine. He is now Manager and Secretary of the Ontario People's Salt & Soda Company, Limited, of Kincardine. He is by occupation a manufacturer. He was Reeve of Bruce Township for four years, and was for one year Deputy-Reeve of Kincardine, and was also for two years Mayor of Kincardine. He was first elected to the House of Commons for the West Riding of Bruce on June 23, 1896. An Independent.—*Kincardine, O.*

HON. N. C. WALLACE.

(West York.)

The Hon. Nathaniel Clarke Wallace was born in Woodbridge, Ont., May 21, 1844. He is the third son of the late Captain Nathaniel Wallace and Ann Wallace, natives of County Sligo, Ireland, who came to Canada in 1834 and 1833 respectively. He was educated in Woodbridge Public School and at the Weston Grammar School. He is a merchant and flour miller. He was Reeve of Vaughan from 1874 to 1879, and was Warden of the County of York in 1878. He was elected for Parliament for West York in 1878, 1882, 1887, 1891, 1892 and in 1896 by 4,068, the largest majority on record in the history of the Dominion. He was Controller of Customs of Canada from December, 1892, until December, 1895, in which year he resigned. He has been Grand Master of the Loyal Orange Association of British America since 1887, and has been President of the Triennial Council of the Orangemen of the World since 1891. A Liberal-Conservative.—*Woodbridge, O.*

URIAH WILSON.

(Lennox.)

Uriah Wilson was born on March 17, 1841, in the Township of North Fredericksburg, County of Lennox and Addington, Ont. His father was a native of England, and his mother name from County Tyrone, Ireland. He was educated at the Public School at Napanee, Ont. In 1867 he married Miss Mary Moyle of Napanee. Mr. Wilson is by occupation a merchant. He represented Centre Ward in the Town Council in 1875, 1876 and 1878, and was Deputy Reeve of Napanee in 1879, 1880, 1881 and 1882; Warden of the County of Lennox and Addington in 1882; Reeve of Napanee in 1884 and 1885, and held the office of Mayor in 1886. He was first elected to the House of Commons at the general elections of 1887, was defeated at the general elections of 1891, but was returned at a by-election held in 1892 and again at the general elections of 1896. A Conservative.—*Napanee, O.*

HON. J. F. WOOD, Q.C., P.C.

(Brockville.)

The Hon. John Fisher Wood was born at Elizabethtown, County of Leeds, Ont., October 12, 1852, and is the son of John Wood, formerly of Dundee, Scotland, and afterwards of Brockville. He was called to the Bar of Ontario in 1876, and was appointed Q.C. in February, 1890. Mr. Wood is Solicitor for the United Counties of Leeds and Grenville, and for the Brockville Loan & Savings Company. He was first elected to the House of Commons at the general elections of 1882, and was re-elected in 1887, 1891 and 1896. In 1890 he was appointed Deputy-Speaker of the Commons and Chairman of Committees, and in 1892 was appointed Chairman of the Committee on Railways and Canals. In December, 1892, he was appointed Comptroller of Inland Revenue and Comptroller of Customs in 1896, but resigned in July, 1896. A Conservative.—*Brockville, O.*

A. T. WOOD.

(Hamilton.)

Andrew Trew Wood was born at Mount Norris, Armagh, Ireland, August, 1826, his father being David Wood. a merchant, whose family originally came from Scotland, and settled there. On the maternal side he is of English descent. He came to Canada in 1846, and married first, in 1851, Mary E., eldest daughter of the late William Freeman, Esq.,of Saltfleet, Ont.; second, 1863, Jennie, eldest daughter of Geo. H. White, Esq., of Yorkville, Ont. He is senior partner of the well-known hardware firm of Wood, Vallance & Co. Among the public offices held by him is that of President of the Hamilton Art School, Director of the Bank of Hamilton, and Vice-President of the Hamilton Provident & Loan Company. Is a Member of the Senate of the University of Toronto and of the Board of Trustees. Has also been President of the Hamilton Board of Trade. He sat in Parliament from the general elections of 1874 to 1878. He stood again at the general elections of 1896, and was successful.—*Hamilton, O.*

JOHN YEO.

(East Prince, P.E.I.)

John Yeo was born at Port Hill, P. E. I., June 29, 1837. He was educated at Uxbridge, England. Mr. Yeo is engaged in business as a merchant and shipowner. In 1870 he was appointed a member of the P.E.I. Executive Council, and in 1871 he was elected Speaker of the House of Assembly. He was elected in June, 1875, Most Worshipful Grand Master of the Freemasons of Prince Edward Island. In 1873 he was reappointed to the Executive Council and also in 1876, but resigned in 1879. He held a seat in the House of Assembly for the 2nd District of Prince from 1858 until 1891, when he resigned in order to become a candidate for the Commons. He was first elected to the Commons at the general elections of 1891 for Prince, and was re-elected for East Prince at that of 1896. A Liberal.—*Porthill, P.E.I.*

J. E. SEAGRAM.

(North Waterloo.)

Joseph Emm Seagram was born in the County of Waterloo, Ont., in 1841. He is the son of Octavius Augustus Seagram and Amelia Styles, who both came from Bratton, Wiltshire, Eng. He was educated at Galt Grammar School, and was married in 1869 to Stephanie Erbs, of Galt, Ont. Mr. Seagram carries on an extensive business as a miller and distiller. He takes an active interest in municipal affairs, and has been a Town Councillor of the thriving town of Waterloo, Ont., where his business is located. He was first returned to Parliament at the general election of 1896 as a Conservative.— *Waterloo, O.*

INDEX.

Name	Page	Name	Page	Name	Page
Adams Hon. M., Q.C.	54	Casey G. E., B.A., J.P.	122	Fortin Thomas	134
Aikins Hon. J. C., P.C.	54	Casgrain Hon. C. E.	68	Foster Hon. G. E., B.A.	166
Allan Hon. G. W., P.C.	55	Casgrain Thomas C.	126	Fraser D. C.	147
Almon Hon. W. J., M.D.	56	Champagne L. N.	129	Fraser John	138
Angers L. C. A.	106	Charlton John	127	Frost Francis T.	128
Armand Lt.-Col. Hon.J.F.	55	Chauvin L. A.	122	Ganong G. W.	132
Bain Thomas	107	Choquette P. A., LL.B.	123	Gauthier Joseph	131
Baird Hon. G. T.	56	Christie Thomas, M.D.	124	Gauvreau C. A.	148
Baker Hon. G. B., M.A.	57	Clancy J.	125	Geoffrion Hon. C. A., Q.C.	37
Bazinet Charles	108	Clarke E. F.	124	Gibson William	145
Beattie Major Thomas	107	Clemow Hon. Francis	96	Gillies J. A., M.A., Q.C.	149
Beausoleil C.	109	Cochrane E., J.P.	123	Gilmour James	150
Beith Robert	110	Cochrane Hon. M. H.	65	Godbout Joseph, M.D.	138
Belcourt N. A.	111	Copp Albert J. S.	125	Gowan Hon. J. R., C.M.G	74
Bell Adam C.	112	Corby Henry	130	Graham Duncan	135
Bell J. W.	113	Costigan Hon. John, J.P.	131	Guay P. M., M.D.	137
Bellerose Hon. J. H.	58	Cowan Mahlon K.	128	Guillet George	152
Bennett W. H.	109	Cox Hon. George A.	67	Guité J. F.	127
Bergeron J. G. H., B.C.L.	106	Craig T. D.	132	Haggart Hon. J G.	146
Bernier Hon. T. A.	64	Dandurand Hon. Raoul.	69	Hale Frederic Hardinge	114
Bernier M. E.	111	Davies Hon. Sir L.H., Q.C.	19	Haley Allen	153
Bertram Geo. H.	108	Davin N. F.	133	Harwood H. S.	141
Bethune J. L., M.D.	112	Davis T. O.	177	Henderson David	139
Blair Hon. A. G., Q.C.	33	De Blois Hon. P. A.	66	Heyd Charles B.	140
Blanchard T.	110	Dechene A. M.	134	Hingston Hon. Sir W. H.	81
Bolduc Hon. Joseph	57	Desmarais Odilon	135	Hodgins W. T.	142
Borden Hon. F. W., M.D.	21	Dever Hon. James	67	Hughes Major Samuel	154
Borden R. L.	116	Dickey Hon. R. B., Q.C.	63	Hurley J. M.	155
Bostock Hewitt	118	Dobell Hon. R. R.	29	Hutchison William	158
Boucher de Boucherville Hon. C. E., M.D.	62	Dobson Hon. John	58	Ingram A. B.	146
Boulton Hon. Lt.-Col. C.A.	59	Domville Lieut.-Col. Jas.	136	Ives Hon. W. B., Q.C.	160
Bourassa J. H. N.	115	Douglas J. M.	136	Jameson R. W.	156
Bourbonnais A., M.D.	115	Drummond Hon. G. A.	63	Joly de Lotbinière Hon. Sir H. G.	41
Bourinot J. G., C.M.G.	103	Dugas J. L. E.	130	Kaulbach Lieut.-Col. C. E.	157
Bowell Hon. Sir M.	61	Dupré Hercule	143	Kendry J.	162
Britton B. M.	114	Dyment A. E.	139	King Hon. G. G.	64
Broder A.	113	Earle Thomas	129	Kirchhoffer Hon. J. N.	79
Brodeur L. P.	114	Edgar Hon. J. D.	101	Klock J. B.	156
Brown J. P.	117	Edwards W. C.	137	Kloepfer Christian	143
Bruneau A. A.	116	Ellis J. V.	142	Landerkin G., M.D.	155
Burnett Leonard	117	Erb D. K.	141	Landry Hon. A. C. P. R.	71
Calvert W. S.	118	Ethier J. A. C.	140	Lang John	154
Cameron M. C., Q.C.	119	Featherston Joseph	144	Langevin E. J., N.P.	51
Campbell Archibald	119	Ferguson Hon. D., P.C.	70	Larivière Hon. A. A. C.	185
Cargill Henry	120	Ferguson John	126	Laurier Rt. Hon. Sir Wilfrid, P.C., K.C.M.G.	11
Carling Hon. Sir John	65	Fiset Hon. J. B. R., M.D.	93	Lavergne Louis	163
Caron Hon. Sir Adolphe	121	Fisher Hon. S. A., B.A.	25	Legris J. H.	153
Carroll Henry G.	121	Fitzpatrick Hon. C., Q.C.	43	Lemieux Adolphe	159
Carscallen A. W.	120	Flint T. B.	161	LeMoyne J. de St. D.	53
Cartwright Hon. Sir R. J.	13	Forget Hon. L. J.	62		

INDEX.

Name	Page
Lewin Hon. J. D	71
Lewis W. J., M.D	164
Lister J. F., Q.C.	148
Livingston J	151
Logan H. J	149
Lougheed Hon. J. A.	70
Lovitt Hon. John	69
Macdonald A. C.	151
Macdonald Hon. A. A.	78
Macdonald Hon. W. J.	73
Macdonald P., M.D.	152
Macdonell J. A.	157
Macfarlane Hon. Alex.	95
MacInnes Hon. D.	73
MacKeen Hon. David	86
MacLaren A. F.	167
MacLean W. F.	159
Macpherson T. H.	158
McAlister J.	160
McCallum Hon. Lachlan.	92
McCarthy D'Alton, Q.C.	165
McCleary William	165
McClure Firman	171
McCormick George	165
McDonald Hon. William.	83
McDougall H. F.	172
McGregor W.	170
McGugan M.	169
McHugh George	147
McInerney G. V.	173
McInnes W. W. B.	170
McIsaac C. F.	171
McKay Hon. Thomas	83
McKindsey Hon. G. C.	84
McLaren Hon. Peter	85
McLennan A., M.D.	176
McLennan Lt.-Col. R. R.	184
McMillan Hon. D., M.D.	78
McMillan J	172
McMullen J	174
McNeil Alexander	174
Mackie T.	150
Madore J. A. C.	193
Malouin A.	161
Marcotte F. A., M.D.	169
Martin Alexander	173
Masson Hon. L. F, R.	72
Maxwell G. R	168
Meigs D. B.	175
Merner Hon. Samuel	80
Mignault R. M. S., M.D.	162
Miller Hon. W., Q.C., P.C.	75
Mills Hon. David, LL.B.	17
Mills J. B., M.A., Q.C.	182
Monet Dominique	183
Monk F. D	180
Montague Hon. W. H.	175
Montplaisir Hon. H.	85
Moore A. H	196
Morin J. B	176
Morrison Aulay, LL.B.	179
Mulock Hon. Wm. Q.C.	23
O'Brien Hon. James	77
O'Donohoe Hon. J., Q.C.	77
Ogilvie Hon. Lt.-Col. A. W.	76
Oliver Frank	182
Osler E. B	177
Owens Hon. W., J.P	72
Parmalee C. H	167
Paterson Hon. Wm	39
Pelletier Hon. C. A. P.	49
Penny E. Goff	164
Petter W. V	165
Poirier Hon. P., M.A.	80
Pope R. H	178
Poupore J.	178
Powell H. A	179
Power Hon. L. G., LL.B.	75
Prefontaine R. F.	180
Price Hon. E. J., D.C.L.	76
Primrose Hon. C.	84
Prior Lt.-Col. Hon. E. G.	181
Proulx Isidore	189
Prowse Hon. Samuel	86
Quinn M. J. F., Q.C.	189
Ratz Valentine	191
Reesor Hon. David	82
Reid Hon. James	89
Reid J. D., M.D.	184
Richardson R. L.	182
Rinfret C. I. M.D.	181
Robertson John R.	186
Robinson James	183
Robitaille Hon. T., M.D.	89
Roche W. J., M.D.	187
Roddick Thomas G., M.D.	190
Rogers David D	191
Rosamond Bennett	187
Ross Hon. J. J., M.D.	90
Ross J A., M.D.	186
Russell Benjamin	192
Rutherford J. G	194
Sanford Hon. W. E.	94
Savard P. V	195
Scott Hon. R. W., Q.C.	15
Scriver J	196
Seagram J. E	206
Semple Andrew	185
Sifton Hon. C., Q.C	35
Smith Hon. Sir F., Knt	91
Smith Lieut.-Col. H. R.	105
Snetsinger J. G	188
Snowball Hon. J. B.	93
Somerville James	197
Sproule T. S., M.D	193
Stenson M. T.	197
Strathcona and Mount Royal, Lord	45
Stubbs W	192
Sullivan Hon. M., M.D.	82
Sutherland Hon. J	50
Sutherland James	198
Talbot O. E	198
Tarte Hon. J. I.	27
Taylor George	199
Temple Hon. Thomas	88
Templeman Hon. W.	91
Thibaudeau Hon. A. A.	92
Thibaudeau Hon. Jos. R.	87
Tisdale Hon. D.	195
Tolmie J.	203
Tucker J. J.	194
Tupper Hon. Sir C., Bart.	201
Tupper Hon. Sir C. H.	202
Turcot George	202
Tyrwhitt Lieut.-Col. R.	199
Vidal Hon. Alex	95
Villeneuve Hon. J. O.	94
Wallace Hon. N. C.	203
Wark Hon. David	66
Wilson Uriah	204
Wood A. T.	205
Wood Hon. J. F., Q.C.	204
Wood Hon. Josiah	87
Yeo John	205

www.ingramcontent.com/pod-product-compliance
Lightning Source LLC
Chambersburg PA
CBHW031818220426
43662CB00007B/704